INSPIRATIONAL STORIES OF HUMAN RESOURCE PROFESSIONALS
LEADING, THRIVING, AND BREAKING BARRIERS

LATINAS
RISING UP
IN HR

PRISCILLA GUASSO

LATINAS RISING UP IN HR

This book is a compilation of stories from numerous people who have each contributed a chapter and is designed to provide inspiration to our readers.

It is sold with the understanding that the publisher and the individual authors are not engaged in the rendering of psychological, legal, accounting or other professional advice. The content and views in each chapter are the sole expression and opinion of its author and not necessarily the views of Fig Factor Media, LLC.

For more information visit: www.latinasrisingupinhr.com

Cover Design & Layout by Juan Manuel Serna
Printed in the United States of America
Fig Factor Media, LLC | www.figfactormedia.com

ISBN: 978-1-952779-18-3
Library of Congress Number: 2020919646

I dedicate this book to our
Latina youth aspiring to achieve
dreams that burn deeply in
their hearts. You are seen and
your leadership is needed
throughout the world.

Table of Contents:

Acknowledgements 6

Introduction 10

Preface by Salvador Mendoza 13

PRISCILLA GUASSO 21

The Journey to What Matters Most

VALERIE HOPE 35

From Surviving to Thriving

NAYSA APARICIO-HERNANDEZ....................................47

Follow Your Dreams Wherever They Go

KATIE LOPES 57

Finding HR

MYRIAM DEL ANGEL..71

Networking Can Help Your Career

MONICA TIJERINA 81

Thanks to Mom

FRANCISCA PHILLIPS...91

Ten Lessons

IRMA I. REYES... 101

Latina Leading with Confidence

KARINA A. JIMENEZ 113

Riding the Waves of Change

SUSANA MOTA 125

When the Stars Align

LUZ PEREZ 135

    Create Your Own Path

PAMELA CARMEN BURGA 147

    My Journey Home

MERCEDES JAIME 159

    Blessings In Disguise

KARINA PRO 171

    Chutes and Ladders

SONYA LAMAS 181

    Overcoming Obstacles: The Path of an HR Rising Star

JANINE TING JANSEN 191

    Diversity, Inclusion and the Corporate Mom

GRISELDA RODRIGUEZ 203

    Working Hard to Never Give Up

STEPHANIE MARTINEZ 213

    From Surviving To Thriving

EDITH PACHECO 225

    Faith, Perseverance, and Resilience

ISABEL MONTES 235

    Finding your Light: A Story of Purpose and Determination

Resources 245

Acknowledgements

"We keep moving forward, opening new doors, and doing new things, because we're curious and curiosity keeps leading us down new paths."

- Walt Disney

One of my day's most beautiful, cherished moments is when I can remove the distractions of endless phone notifications and listen intently to the wisdom from my Abuelita Isabel Espinosa and Grandma Agueda Bernal Alvarado. In every conversation, I take away so much from their more than eighty years of life and am inspired to learn that who I am today is a result of all the ups and downs they have each experienced, either in Mexico or the U.S. I am blessed to have them both in my life, teaching me the importance of family and encouraging me to never stop being curious and taking advantage of opportunities as they come.

To my dad, Adrian Alvarado: You have taught me more than you know. You have always believed in me, pushing me to reach as high as I want to go. I've been blessed to have you there encouraging me to take a step back and take care of myself. I couldn't be prouder to be your daughter and thank you for being there to support me during some of my toughest times.

To my *mami,* Isabel Estrada, and step-father Fredy

Salas: You both have been my cheerleaders, never letting a day go by without sharing how proud you are of your daughters and reminding us to trust that God looks out for us. Thank you for showing me how to lead with my heart, never forgetting who I am and where I come from.

To my younger sister, Mia Salas: Thank you for the privilege of not just being your older sister, but for reminding me not to take life too seriously. You are one of the driving forces in why I do what I do and love you more than you know.

To my sister, Jessica Galvan: As I shared in my story, you have always been one of the constant pillars in my life. I am so thankful for your serving heart and how you've been right there next to me when I needed it most. Thank you for challenging, encouraging, and supporting me to focus on me. You've taught me so much and I wouldn't be who I am if you weren't in my life. "No matter how far apart we are, a string forever holds our hearts together." - A & E

To my brother-in-law, Gerardo Galvan: Thank you for your (& Jess') support this past year when Covid hit and welcoming Jorge, Cocoa and I into your home for 6 months without hesitation. I see you as a brother and promise to invite you to our wedding vow renewal. ;)

To my littles: Elena, Ari, Ollie, and Ellie: You four inspire me to live life to the fullest and to never take a day for granted. Never forget how amazingly gifted you each are and that you have the ability to do whatever gives your heart joy.

To my Alvarado, Espinosa, Guasso and Bernal family: We have a beautiful connection that expands globally. Thank you for your ongoing love and support. Each of our families have so much to give to this world and celebrate. Thank you for the gift of family and unconditionally loving me and Jorge.

To my amazing friend, mentor, and ex-boss Salvador Mendoza: Thank you for leaning into your curiosity and giving me my break all those years ago. We need more leaders like you who are making an impact in the Latino community and beyond. I can't thank you and the Mendoza family enough for treating us like family, encouraging me in the creation of this book, and reminding me that everything happens for a reason.

To all my past colleagues, friends, board members, mentors, and previous bosses: Thank you for being a part of my journey and leaving a mark in my life.

To the 19 phenomenal contributing authors that trusted me: Thank you! Together we created something so beautiful that I believe will inspire all walks of life for years to come. May we always remain connected sharing the drive to make a change in this world.

To Jackie Camacho-Ruiz, Gaby Hernández Franch,

Karen Dix, and the Fig Factor Media team: Thank you for your tireless efforts in coordinating, creating, editing, and ongoing patience with bringing this dream of mine to a reality. You each have impacted our lives in more ways than you know.

To my husband, Jorge Guasso: It's not a secret that in all that I have accomplished, you were the one by my side always believing in my talents and saying "You can do anything!" My life would be nowhere near where it is today without your love, constant support, and grounding influence. Thank you for taking on my dreams as your own. I'm excited for us to now take on your dreams together. *Te amo.*

To my heavenly Father up above: Thank you for blessing me with dreams and moments of hardships where you molded me to be who I am today. In each challenge, I grew, yet you never left my side. Thank you for teaching me that I will continue to be a work in progress. Please bless those in this book and create a wave of inspiration in the lives of those who read it. "For everything there is a season…" Ecclesiastes 3:1-8

Introduction

We don't always have the ability to take a moment in our lives to honestly pause, reflect, and create. Prior to the 2020 pandemic, I will never forget the divine moment I had with Jackie Camacho-Ruiz, a long-lost friend of more than twenty years, and now publisher of this book. We reminisced on our inner dreams and values of helping others, while sharing some of the deepest challenges that created speed bumps in our journey. I remember writing down on a napkin what we discussed: a way to open doors and share my knowledge of having attained my dream of becoming an HR executive, vulnerably sharing the personal knowledge I had acquired throughout this journey, and creating a specific platform where Latinas in HR can continue to give back to each other and our youth.

Almost nine months later, through this labor of heartfelt passion, gratitude, and inspiration, I'm excited to bring to the world the beginning of this dream: an anthology consisting of twenty stories of Latina HR professionals. As you read, may you see them not only for their professional accolades, but be encouraged by their resilience, vulnerability, and determination to attain their dreams for themselves and their families.

You may ask, why is it important to call out the success of Latinas Rising Up In HR and open the doors to what their experiences have been? While I believe and see the U.S. as a land of opportunity for many, we cannot overlook the statistics. We must collectively push for new leadership by holding organizations and each other accountable with investing in the development of Latina leaders.

- 4% of executive positions at Fortune 100 companies are held by Latinas.[1]

- 2% of board seats are held by Latinas.[2]

- The U.S. Hispanic population reached 60.6 million in 2019, up from 50.7 million in 2010.[3]

- Latinas make up 10.3% total US employees in 2019.[4]

- 18% of the workforce is of Hispanic descent with anticipation of increasing to 29% by 2060.[5]

- Projected by Catalyst Research: 28.7% of the workforce from 2018-2028 will be Hispanic Women.[6]

- 4.3% of Latinas hold management positions.[7]

- Latinas earn 54 cents for every dollar earned by a white, non-Hispanic man.[8]

[1] Missing Pieces Report. 2018. catalyst.org. https://www.catalyst.org/wp-content/uploads/2019/01/missing_pieces_report_01152019_final.pdf.

[2] Minkel, Alida. "2019 HACR CII Report Data Snapshot: Governance." HACR Blog Home. HACR Hispanic Association on Corporate Responsibility , 2019. https://www.blog.hacr.org/hri_blog/2019-hacr-cii-snapshot-governance?utm_term=2020_HACR_HRI_Gov

[3] Noe-Bustamante, Luis, Mark Hugo Lopez, and Jens Manuel Krogstad. "U.S. Hispanic Population Surpassed 60 Million in 2019, but Growth Has Slowed." Pew Research Center. Pew Research Center, July 10, 2020. https://www.pewresearch.org/fact-tank/2020/07/07/u-s-hispanic-population-surpassed-60-million-in-2019-but-growth-has-slowed/.

[4] Catalyst. 2020. Women of Color in the United States: Quick Take. Catalyst. https://www.catalyst.org/research/women-of-color-in-the-united-states/

[5] Employed Persons by Occupation, Race, Hispanic or Latino Ethnicity, and Sex, January 22, 2020. https://www.bls.gov/cps/cpsaat10.htm.

[6] 2018 HACR Corporate Inclusion Index. Hispanic Alliance of Corporate Responsibility, 2018.

[7] Catalyst. 2020. Women of Management: Quick Take. Catalyst. https://www.catalyst.org/research/women-in-management/

[8] The Wage Gap: The Who, How, Why, and What To Do." NWLC. National Women's Law Center , July 21, 2020. https://nwlc.org/resources/the-wage-gap-the-who-how-why-and-what-to-do/

In reviewing this data, it is clear to see that much work is needed in all facets when it comes to representation of Latinas and People of Color. In HR, we can influence a change of thought and challenge our organizations to do more. Ultimately, we still have so much work to do in building greater representation for Latinas in upper management. Collectively, lets act on further inspiring and encouraging our youth, recruiting and developing the approximate ten percent of Latinas that make up the U.S. workforce, and investing in leadership skills of Latinas. HACR has published that over the past five years, executive-level representation of Latinas has remained below two percent. That is just unacceptable. I believe in the importance of representation and if we can further diversify our HR teams to reflect those they support on the frontline; a new set of leadership will emerge.

In the Reflect and Rise micro-mentoring moments following each chapter, our contributing authors offer advice to encourage you in your personal and professional journey. I invite you to read one story every week and reflect on how these Latinas Rising Up In HR are defying the statistical odds. Send them words of encouragement on LinkedIn for being authentic to who they are, where they come from, what their families have taught them, and how they are excelling every day. May this be a reminder about the importance and responsibility we each have to share our keys of opportunity and knowledge to inspire others to keep rising up.

PREFACE
By Salvador Mendoza
NBC Universal

I remember it was Thanksgiving 2005, and I was the VP of Diversity & Inclusion of Hyatt Hotels. I was sitting in my office at the corporate headquarters when the phone rang. It was security saying I had an unannounced visitor who wanted to speak with me. She was a college student at the University of Illinois Urbana-Champaign business school who had seen my name in an article about diversity. She wanted to talk to me about my profession and getting into the industry.

As I've always appreciated young people who take initiative in seeking out mentors, I was intrigued and decided to give her a few minutes. I told security to send her to the café, grabbed my jacket, and headed downstairs. I walked in, and there was Priscilla Guasso.

I was instantly struck by her high-energy and enthusiasm, which years later, remain contagious to those around her. At that time, Priscilla was thinking about being a wedding/event planner, but she had also worked within several multi-cultural programs at the university. I liked her energy, so I put her in contact with the catering manager at two of our Chicagoland hotels and told her to stay in touch.

A year later, when Priscilla made her way into HR at the Hyatt Regency O'Hare, she popped on my radar again. Then our paths crossed at a regional HR meeting—a leadership development gathering where many important, cross-functional contacts are made. There was a position on my team which I thought would interest her, but not wanting to poach from my colleague, I wanted Priscilla to approach me. She did.

For a time, the Diversity & Inclusion (D&I) department was just the two of us and I greatly appreciated her "can do", "will do", "will find a way" and resourceful attitude. She ultimately continued to grow her career, managed imperative partnerships with external organizations and influenced employee morale through the management of our Global Diversity Council. She also launched the inaugural five Employee Resources Groups (ERGs). Priscilla continued to move her HR career quickly up the corporate ladder in hospitality and healthcare as a well-respected corporate executive while also pursuing advocacy within D&I by having joined different boards such as the National Hispanic Corporate Council (NHCC), Mujeres de HACE (Hispanic Alliance for Career Enhancement) board, and University of Illinois' Latino Latina Alumni board. It is a privilege and an honor to further support her advocacy with the launch of this book and her future success with building, connecting, and coaching a community of Latina HR professionals.

Diversity, Equity & Inclusion (DEI)
Today at NBC Universal

As I reflect, the foundation for my own personal journey within diversity began when I migrated to this country from Honduras at the age of fourteen, not knowing the language and having to adapt to a new culture in Chicago's south side. In college, I aligned myself with organizations that helped Latinos. I've been lucky and have found mentors along the way. Now, I report to work at the iconic 30 Rockefeller Plaza building every day, always grateful for the opportunities that led me there.

I arrived at NBCUniversal in 2012 as vice president of Diversity, Equity & Inclusion during an exciting time for our country – hopeful and on the cusp of potential change and in an important election year, just as we are now. President Obama was seeking his second term and immigration was a hot issue, as it is now. As in previous years, there were demands that the American media stop using the derogatory phrase, "illegal aliens" as a descriptor of the immigrant community. In short time, I learned that in direct response, NBC News' executive leadership and the executive vice president & chief diversity officer were working to change such a derogatory phrase that had slithered its way into the American lexicon. I am proud to say that NBC was the first major network to change the narrative and started using the phrase, "undocumented immigrants," which is a more accurate depiction of the community's condition in America. The policy change was to extend to all network and local newscasts, stations, special programming, and requiring hosts to politely correct their guests who may use the outmoded phrase. I was proud of my company for leading the way with this change and I felt validated that I had joined the right organization. I was even happier when I began noticing how this considerate turn of phrase caught on with (well, most) the other networks. In one fell swoop, the policy change had validated the responsibility of media and entertainment to provide the right narrative on this issue to the country, and validated how we, as a company, were playing a part of such an important change.

This example shows how language is important, as is our personal story with diversity, as we attempt to create a culture of DE&I, not only in our workplace, but also in our world. Today, diversity is on everyone's mind, and we all want to get it right. In the corporate world, I see that most senior leaders and executives are committed and see the strategy behind it, but they often struggle to get started. My role is to help them discover where they are in their diversity journey and discerning how I can provide the resources needed to make changes. It's important because DE&I has become a competitive advantage for many organizations. So much so that I have noticed a definitive shift in the last six months as to how it is manifesting in our businesses.

First, employees are feeling more empowered to raise their voice, and executive leadership has provided a safe space to do that. I see the rise of networking and employee resource groups, in particular from Black and Latino colleagues, and HR is at the heart of listening, serving these communities, and shepherding this empowerment. It's also important that we emphasize that ignorance about DE&I issues is an opportunity for education, not hostility.

The second trend I am seeing is allyship. White, senior level executives are seeking ways to support DE&I within their organizations, they are saying, "I see you!", "I hear you!", "I am with you!". In the past six months I have received many calls from executives within the company asking how they can engage and support our efforts.

In other words, where once I felt the momentum of DE&I, I now see it as a movement that's here to stay. However, I am a cautious person by nature, so I emphasize that caution must be taken to ensure that raising our voices comes from a place of EMPOWERMENT, rather than ENTITLEMENT. Among my purview is managing ninety ERG chapters with almost fifteen thousand employees and more than two hundred leaders who share that caution.

Investing in Latina HR Leadership

Meanwhile, access to opportunity must be advocated for all minorities, and in the field of HR, which I see as the moral center of all companies, I think Latinas are a particular asset. As the authors in this book illustrate, Latinas are intuitive, empathic, and also possess the grit, determination, and business savvy leadership to succeed. They are natural creators of culture and unite those around them. They have the gifted combination of strategic, results-driven thinking and the soft skills and emotional intelligence needed to work with a diverse group on a personal level. Often, access to mentorship is their biggest challenge, but that can take all shapes and forms, even stories like those shared in this book.

When I coach people, I tell them to do what I have done—prepare yourself and find opportunity. When one stands before you, don't concentrate on the pay or recognition which comes with it. Instead, consider how the opportunity expands your network and helps your skillset. Does it prepare you for exponential growth? Does the opportunity prepare you for two, three, or five years into the future? Will you be able to say you were part of something great?

At networking meetings, don't introduce yourself by your title; tell people what you do and how you are making a difference. And be genuine. We all can tell when a person really likes us or is trying to get something from us. Connect authentically, because the most important part of human resources is truly the humanity of it.

We are now in the midst of a pandemic, in which we have been forced to distance ourselves from each other. In the corporate world, the spotlight is shining heavily upon our technical support, rather than human resources. This makes it an even more opportune time for a book like this to enter the world. It reminds us that even at a social distance, our strength is in our resiliency to adapt to changing times. Our efforts in diversity illustrate this, as well as the stories from all of the professionals in this book. We have quite a way to go in diversifying talent throughout management and executive and board roles in corporate America, but each year we continue to make incremental change, and that is to be celebrated.

Congratulations to all the authors!

SALVADOR MENDOZA
Vice President, Diversity, Equity & Inclusion
NBC Universal

THE JOURNEY TO WHAT MATTERS MOST

BY PRISCILLA GUASSO

"Take chances, boldly invest in yourself, and give yourself permission to pause."

My family and friends have always described me as a person with a contagious energy and spark in the way I speak, laugh, and get things done. Honestly, I never thought much about it because in high school, I considered myself a quiet, social butterfly. I loved meeting new people and learned so much by listening and watching others. However, I never had one solid group of friends, nor a hobby or mission that guided my life. All I knew was that I would continue focusing on doing whatever felt right and brought me joy.

At home, my dad and mom worked tirelessly to provide us with the basics in life and so much more. My mom came to the U.S. from Mexico to start a life with my dad whose parents emigrated here from Mexico. My dad was born in the U.S. but spent countless months between both countries, so I learned to speak Spanish at home and English at school. My dad showed me the power that an education and a well-thought plan can bring into your life. I saw him become increasingly successful from countless work opportunities which supported our moves from an apartment, to a townhouse, to a house, and finally, to what felt like a real-life Barbie dreamhouse. My mom is my life cheerleader and never let a day go by without a kiss on the cheek and an encouraging word. While my parents are not together anymore, they have humbly taught me valuable lessons of balance, humility, love, and perseverance. We remain close to this day.

SEIZING OPPORTUNITIES

Growing up, I always felt pressure to become "something." It was never an expectation that anyone put on me; rather, it was because I did not see anyone like me represented in school or the media. As my dad climbed the corporate ladder, my parents put my younger sister and me in bigger and better schools. I was always on the go, never afraid to be the "new girl," and ready to make new friends wherever I started. Over time, as I grew confident in who I was becoming and my purpose, that quiet social butterfly's voice grew much louder.

While my high school was predominantly white, I found

myself constantly dreaming of traveling and learning about other cultures firsthand. After school and on weekends, I spent my time at my church where the congregation was all Latino, and everyone spoke Spanish. I bounced back and forth between different worlds, learning from everyone who crossed my path. Then I met a high school teacher named Mr. Correa, who shared his cultural pride through language, food, and music. I finally felt I could openly share the pride I had in my Mexican roots while in school. I began unfolding a beautiful secret I was holding deep inside for so long -- I am Mexican American. He opened my eyes to how beautiful both cultures are and encouraged us to share that with the world. Together, we built a small Latino club with no more than twenty students where we would speak in English and Spanish, eat delicious food, laugh at stories, talk about faith, dreams, and just be in community.

One day, he asked if anybody wanted to go on a field trip to the U.S. Hispanic Leadership Institute's (USHLI) High School Leadership Conference. I jumped at the opportunity because I wanted to meet more people like me. Representation matters so much. At the conference, I heard speakers who inspired my soul and added greater fuel to my dreams. I immediately felt connected with one of the main speakers, who had a similar story to mine. Her experience showed the young crowd to ignore the statistics and to keep fighting hard for your dreams. There she was, a professionally dressed businesswoman, understanding our different walks of life and firing off nothing but affirmations and encouragement. I realized that I too wanted to inspire others like me, but first I had to believe it, create it, and take many leaps of faith.

Life continued to bring challenges, with thoughts of feeling like I was never enough. Oddly, this propelled me to take chances. During college, I thought I was going to finish with a computer science degree. After almost failing a few classes that I worked so hard to pass, and crying on the bathroom floor, my boyfriend (now husband) believed in me and encouraged me not to give up. We created a new plan focusing on going into business, and he introduced me to an amazing angel, University of Illinois' College of Business Assistant Dean, Jewell White. The dean took the time to help me see what my options were; he was honest in his feedback and guided me on what I needed to do to successfully transfer schools. I focused on my job as a resident advisor, supporting a floor of ladies who chose to explore topics of culture, race, gender, ethnicity, disabilities, and more. With the support of my husband, family, and mentors, I proudly graduated with a degree in business with a concentration in marketing. However, without specific experience in the field, obtaining a job was going to be much more difficult.

In the preface, my amazing professional mentor, Sal, shared how I literally showed up at his office, inspiring him with my motivation and resolve to work for an amazing company. Through his guidance and the mentorship of many other leaders, I continued to move quickly up the company ladder, averaging what felt like one promotion every year. I was speeding through roles that taught me about all the areas in HR: benefits, recognition, employment, employee relations, layoffs, workman's compensation, etc. Each role sharpened my leadership toolkit on emotional intelligence, learning the business, becoming a strategic partner, motivating through inspiration, and connecting to others. I was not only learning leadership skills from the professionals around me, but they were also sharing their life with me. I truly believe God placed each one of them in my life at different seasons to teach me and inspire me to do more.

I remember consulting my colleagues Scott, Colleen, Kristy, Randy, and Doug about making a professional move from Chicago to Miami. Each of them provided me with a different perspective. I was hesitant to move because I wanted to stay closer to my family. They listened, challenged, and encouraged me to go. My husband and I made that move to Miami and through my new role in talent acquisition, I continued to pursue my childhood dream of traveling as I visited almost all of the Latin America and Caribbean teams. I supported and met thousands of people who I'm honored to be connected to today. I am thankful to have had the chance to learn the diversity and richness of cultures throughout each country firsthand. I grew my career in the Diversity, Equity and Inclusion (DE&I) space, ultimately achieving my goal to become a corporate HR executive. Looking back at the employment stats and putting together the applications for DE&I awards, it hit me like a ton of bricks that not everyone readily had mentors and sponsors advocating and investing in their professional and personal development. I also noticed that as I moved up the ladder as a Latina, I was very much the exception. I wanted to become part of the solution for creating a tomorrow where leaders in diverse groups could thrive and positively influence these white spaces. This thinking fueled me, and I began to align my time with organizations that were helping the Latino community that I loved so dearly.

Being on the National Hispanic Corporate Council (NHCC) board for two years connected me with a group of senior Latin@ executives in different companies who created a safe space professionally, but also became forever friends. My "NHCC *viejitas*" is an informal community of ladies and sisterhood where we cheer each other on, challenge our way of thinking, and support each other through life-altering events. My training with the Hispanic Alliance of Career Enhancement's Mujeres de HACE program connected me with Latina professionals across the U.S., like me, looking to expand their careers and build greater visibility of Latina leadership. The Latinista also built a foundation for me to network with ladies in creative fields, fueling my mind with innovative ideas and encouraging me with new skills outside the realm of my corporate network. Finally, my work with University of Illinois' Latino/Latina Alumni Association created a community of encouragement and a platform to connect with college students and graduates as they embarked on their journey. I had achieved so much professionally, and I was very proud of my professional accolades. But my rise only looked easy. I had to simultaneously overcome many obstacles to get where I am today, and because I strive to embody honest, authentic communication, I will share some of the experiences that shaped who I am today.

FINDING INTENTION

In my desired life plan, I had so much focus on moving up the career ladder that I began neglecting important pillars to my foundation and values. I allowed myself to be influenced by leaders who weren't aligned to my values and I slowly learned how to bounce back from this. With all my travel, I was enjoying the opportunities, hyper focused on the next shiny role, neglecting what was most important to me: my husband, my health, our finances, and my values.

About eight years ago, my husband and I were struggling to get ourselves out of thousands of dollars of school and miscellaneous debt. We were previously living outside of our means, charging vacations and dinner dates on credit, and not realizing we were digging ourselves into a deeper and deeper hole. Going out with friends and family became stressful, and we desperately tried to keep our payments going. Together, we agreed to follow a financial program provided through our church. While it was very difficult to tighten our belts, learning to do more with less was essential, and we focused on having financial freedom so we could attain the other dreams we had together.

Then, two years ago, I reached my dream of becoming an HR corporate executive and reporting two levels away from the CEO. I was at an important company conference, meeting leaders from all over the nation for the first time, when I found myself alone in my hotel room experiencing a miscarriage that brought my world crashing down. At the time, I went numb, not fully understanding what was happening. I remember convincing myself to be "strong", inexplicably didn't call a doctor or close family or friend and pushed forward to finish my participation in that conference. At one point I recall time freezing, giving myself very little permission to feel, process, and mourn. Deep inside, I was devastated, furious at what happened, feeling like a failure, and beating myself up for thinking that I got what I deserved for not taking care of my physical health. My miscarriage became a shameful secret that I chose to carry alone, refusing to speak about it with my husband or family and bring to light.

A year later, we suffered a second miscarriage and because I never addressed my inner emotions during the first one it sent me into a downward spiral physically, mentally, emotionally, and spiritually. I leaned on the support of my husband, family, colleagues, and amazing therapists who helped me process, rebuild, focus and once again, find my light that was slowly blowing out in the wind. I vividly remember the day my sister jumped on the first flight out of Chicago to Miami and spent the week with me after an excruciating D&C surgery which was necessary after the miscarriage. She was our rock, lifting us up and ever present with us. As I accepted help from therapy, church, and family, I slowly regained my confidence, grit, and faith. I began to appreciate life at a whole new level and refocused on living with intention through my actions, money, time, and relationships. This meant rebuilding our foundation. We headed back home to Chicago.

My husband supported me on this intentional journey, and we continued with our newfound financial stability and saved for those rainy days that were sprinkled throughout our life thereafter. I was blessed to have family and friends willingly support my dream financially to experience a week-long mission trip through Soul City Church (the church I love) to El Salvador. Originally, I thought our goal was to give back and show God's love by helping paint a school. Little did I know that the kids and families would burrow their way deep into my heart, encourage me to let go of the control I felt I needed, and open my eyes to how we create ripples in each other's lives. I witnessed this through mornings of singing and dancing with the children of the school, afternoons eating lunch with an elderly couple who shared honest marriage advice, and evenings of reflecting and conversing with the encouraging women on the trip.

A PAUSE

I returned from the mission trip refreshed and with even greater focus. Two months later, my husband supported me to take a leap of faith and take a pause on being "Priscilla, the aspiring HR executive" and use 2020 as a year to focus on myself, my health, and this passion project.

I am extremely grateful for the privilege of having a career, but have learned that you receive so much more in life by elevating others. While I continue to have big goals, we go through different seasons in life. Let's be real; it's a struggle to work at relationships when you're trying to keep all the balls up in the air from dropping on the floor. However, the best remedy I've found is to listen to those whispers, courageously act on them, and be specific with the help you give and ask for. It takes a village to achieve any kind of greatness and by genuinely partnering with others, you share those successes and triumphs together.

I represent a proud lineage of family from the U.S. and Mexico that persevered through life's greatest obstacles and because of them, I am here today. While in my head I had a certain plan for my life, I'm now learning to listen to God's whispers and evaluate the pulse of my financial, spiritual, mental, and physical health. Take chances, boldly invest in yourself, and give yourself permission to pause. There is a bigger plan out there for each of us, so let go of your fears and remember we are all mosaics: perfectly imperfect and meant to shine brightly. As I openly share only a small piece of my story with you, my hope is that together we inspire a new wave of leadership inside and outside the Latina community and share the keys of knowledge that will open doors that were previously closed.

REFLECT AND RISE

- **Leaving a legacy:** Unfortunately, when we leave this world, we cannot take any possessions with us. Think hard on what kind of legacy you would like to leave behind. How do others feel and think when you leave a conversation?

- **Grace and resilience are key:** As HR professionals it is so easy to get caught in the whirlwind at home and with work, especially now with COVID-19. Be kind to yourself. Encourage yourself as you do to others and give yourself grace. You're working to achieve your dreams and are bound to run into doors that are locked.

- **Choose gratitude and show it often:** As you move up in your career, hold tight to the people who have been there for you. Take out your phone and text three people that have helped raise you up. Share what their relationship means to you. Do this once a month with family, friends, and coworkers.

- **Positive Visuals:** Find one quote, verse, affirmation, poem, message, or song that can help bring you back to your why. Post it somewhere you can see it every day.

- **Share and build community:** Write your big dreams down and share them out loud with two people that believe in you. Take that bold step forward and if you do not have anyone to share them with, join a community of people who are willing to share a copy of their keys for you to open other doors.

- **Continuously dream and create:** Even the best of plans will present detours. What is that one dream you had as a kid that you let go of that still makes you smile? What is one way you can remain connected to that feeling? Tap into this consistently.

BIOGRAPHY

Based in both Chicago and Miami, Priscilla Guasso thrives in leading human resource teams focused on all areas of the employee life cycle: talent acquisition, mobility, talent development, succession planning, performance management, employee relations, global diversity, equity and inclusion, and overall company culture. Her fifteen years of experience expands to HR in the U.S., Latin America, and the Caribbean in the hospitality and healthcare industry. She enjoys coaching others to invest in themselves and further grow their leadership skills in corporate, nonprofit, and government sectors. As a contributing author and founder of *Latinas Rising Up In HR,* she is focused on building a community that openly shares connections, best practices, and experiences while also giving back to our youth.

Priscilla holds a Bachelor of Science degree in business administration with a concentration in marketing from the University of Illinois Urbana-Champaign. Outside of work, she is an active board member and secretary for HACE's Mujeres de HACE Chicago, membership director of the Latino/Latina Alumni Association for University of Illinois, an inspiration agent for Young Latina Day, member of the HRHotspot, Society of Human Resources Management (SHRM), the National Hispanic Corporate Council (NHCC), and The Latinista. She enjoys traveling to new cities with her husband, Jorge, and soaking up the sun in warmer climates.

Priscilla Guasso

Speaker, Author and HR Leader

Years in HR: 15

Priscilla@LatinasRisingUpInHR.com

Linkedin.com/in/priscillaguasso/

IG: @LatinasInHR @PGuasso

Fb: Latinas Rising Up in HR

FROM SURVIVING TO THRIVING

BY VALERIE HOPE

"We have the silver lining in our minds."

In October of 2008, I flew to Chicago to interview and do a presentation to earn my dream job: regional director of learning for Hyatt Hotels and Resorts. Members of the current corporate learning team, the director, and the vice president of learning were my audience.

I killed it! After the presentation, everyone congratulated me for my delivery and content. The vice president of learning told me to keep an eye out, as they would call me back soon with an offer. I returned home to Dallas, Texas and shared the great news with my family, friends, and colleagues.

My career with Hyatt had begun in 2003, and little did I know that I would be doing some of my best work within the organization. I started out as a training manager for two hotels, and by 2006, I was the area recruiter for the three, full-service properties in the Dallas area. During conversations with my supervisors, I regularly expressed my desire to focus on roles which would allow me to focus on developing leaders. The regional director of learning role was a dream come true!

THE WAIT

I couldn't wait for the call from the corporate office with the job offer. The first week passed and I didn't hear anything. The second week passed, with still no news.

"Jonathan, have you heard any news from the corporate office about my job offer?" I asked my human resources director, Jonathan Chaplowe, "They said they would call in a week. It's been two weeks already."

"No, I haven't heard anything yet," he replied. He recommended I follow up with an email to check in with the VP. I sent an email right away and the response was, "We're reviewing our staffing plan right now and working through the budget; please give us a little while longer."

November came around, with still no news. I reached out again. The response this time was, "Due to the economy, we're going to temporarily freeze all hiring. Unfortunately, we won't be filling that position this year." I felt so disappointed, my thought was, *I'll get it. It's all about the right timing. I can wait until things begin to look up again.*

December rolled around and Jonathan called me into his office on a Friday morning.

"Valerie, things are not looking good financially for the hotel," he said. "We're moving into business planning-mode and we need to stop hiring right away."

I nodded my head in agreement. It made sense. Why continue recruiting if there were no jobs to be had?

"Ok, what would you like me to focus on in the meantime?"

"Well, that's the other thing," he said in a quiet, yet serious tone of voice. "We also need to make changes to our current staffing model. Since we're not hiring, we'll need to look at other options for you too, but I've called the other area hotels and they're all halting the hiring/recruiting process." He paused. "Valerie, I know this is hard to hear, but there aren't any other HR roles here in Dallas."

"Do you mean I'm out of a job?" I asked. He nodded and sighed. "What about the assistant HR director (AHRD) position that we've been trying to fill for these past weeks? Is that a role I could take?"

He told me he'd already had someone in the pipeline, and they would likely be moving forward with that candidate. He said he was puzzled that I would even bring it up, since I had made it clear in the past that I was not interested in becoming an HR director.

"True, but I want to work here," I responded. He shook his head. I already knew he was committed to developing the assistant to replace him and that was not my preferred career path. He was right. I wanted to continue my work developing leaders and thought the AHRD would be too focused on the administrative functions of HR. At first glance, it was not aligned with my strengths or long-term interests. I was in a daze, which slowly built into a panic.

He recommended I start looking for other positions in the hotels in other cities in Texas. I was shocked and mostly silent the rest of the conversation as my mind raced, thinking through everything he was saying and what it all meant. He was very empathetic and asked that I take the weekend to think about it, and that he would support me in whatever I decided. Monday we would speak again about my decision.

I was a nervous-wreck the entire day. I felt as if all eyes were on me. I was so self-conscious that when I walked into a room and people fell quiet, I just knew they were talking about me! That evening, I called my mom and told her the sad news. She was surprised, but in her never-flagging positivity, she tried to cheer me up and pointed out the positive aspect of potentially finding something new and interesting. It was difficult to receive it. I wasn't ready for that yet.

To make everything even more difficult, the next

day our human resources department was hosting the annual family holiday party. I was the emcee. I facilitated the games, coordinated music with the DJ, joked with our colleagues, and met their families for four hours. It was a temporary escape from the maelstrom in my head, but not an effective one. Although I was assured that no one besides me and Jonathan knew of our conversation the day before, I felt vulnerable and even embarrassed pretending that everything was okay. I couldn't tell anyone at work how anxious and panicked I was feeling, especially when they expressed such enthusiasm about the event, and started to give me ideas and recommendations for the next time. I thought to myself, *what next time? I won't be here for a next time.*

THE SHIFT

When I got home, I called my younger brother, Ricardo, and shared the news about my potential lay-off. As a Marine Corps officer, his brain was perpetually in strategic, problem-solving mode. He asked about my ideas for other jobs within the company, and I told him there weren't any, and that I also didn't want to move to another state and start over.

As we thought through the options, he asked, "So what about the assistant director position? Why aren't you applying for that?"

I explained the role and how it didn't align with my career goals and Jonathan's vision for that position.

"Well, it seems like this would be the prime time to have an internal candidate for that role," said Ricardo. "If they are downsizing, why would they want to relocate someone and retrain them?"

I paused for a moment and thought about what he just said. He challenged me to see how the role and the financial constraints of the company provided a great opportunity to polish and elevate my skills. As we talked, we came up with an idea.

A few months before, I'd completed an online assessment called Strengthsfinder and loved it. So much in fact that I talked many of my friends and family into taking it too. After my conversation with Ricardo, I started to see how I might use those results to match up my talents to the potential role. It was perfect!

I spent the remainder of the weekend mapping my talents and strengths to the key responsibilities in the AHRD job description and tied my candidacy to how it would save the hotel money in relocation expenses, onboarding, and relationship-building.

When I walked into Jonathan's office on Monday, I felt confident and prepared to make a case for why I was the right person for the job. I read Jonathan my list of strengths with examples of how he had seen those strengths in action in my current role and what they would look and sound like in action as the assistant HR director. After I was done talking, he just sat back and stared at me.

"Wow. I was not expecting this," he said with a surprised look on his face. "You've given me even more to think about."

At the end of the day, Jonathan called me back into his office, after discussing it with the general manager.

"I appreciate what you shared," he said. "We think it might be possible, but we still need to talk through how to make the budget work."

"Jonathan, how about you give me six months in the role?" I quickly responded. "You don't have to change my current salary or title in the system. If you don't like what I do in those six months, we'll look for something else and I'll move on."

I had made him an offer he couldn't refuse. He looked me straight in the eye and said, "Ok, let's do it!"

THE DREAM

At the time I struck that deal with Jonathan, I had no idea what this new experience would do for me or the rest of the team. I had already experienced the power of connecting to my own strengths and there was still much to do. We now only had four people on our team doing the work of eight. Our friends had been laid off. Morale was low. Our HR team engagement scores were low. We started by holding several meetings to discuss our engagement action plan.

After speaking with Jonathan, I told him that I would like to be responsible for leadership development for our team. He agreed to let me lead. After consulting with the team, we embarked on a six-week Strengthsfinder series, using "Marcus Buckingham's Trombone Player Wanted" DVDs. Each week, we would watch an episode together, discuss it and do an activity. It was transformative.

We became specialists, rather than generalists. We not only became aware of our own strengths, but we started to rely upon and request each other's strengths in support of our specific projects. It wasn't unusual for Jonathan to call us into a meeting and say, "We need to put together the plan for employee appreciation week. Valerie, you're great with coming up with ideas and we need to come up with meaningful, low-cost ones. Danielle, we need your talent for organizing the details and arranging the calendar. Melissa, your gift for crafting the right message and preparing the signage will be the perfect way to inform the hotel staff." The project was a hit, as were many other major initiatives. We had created our own HR version of Ocean's 11!

I worked in that role for a year and a half. One

morning, Jonathan called me into his office as soon as I walked through the door. He told me the VP of HR at the corporate office called and asked if I was still interested in being a regional director of learning. If so, the job was mine. I was offered the job I had interviewed for a year and a half earlier, without going through the interview process again. Of course, I accepted!

This experience taught me three lessons. First, it taught me the importance of reaching out to those around me who have different perspectives and who can listen deeply to what I truly needed. Secondly, I learned what a gift it is for us all to channel our energy and creativity into our strengths and talents. Doing this helped Jonathan see what I could offer the team. Lastly, even in a situation in which I had little control and I felt uncomfortable, I learned to connect to a deeper purpose and meaning. I needed to be humble enough to seek to learn, challenge, and reinvent myself.

We must shift how we look at our challenges. We have the silver lining in our minds.

REFLECT AND RISE

The Swiss psychiatrist, Carl Jung, said "He who looks outside, dreams. He who looks inside, awakens." It's our responsibility to OWN, MASTER, and GIVE AWAY our strengths. What I like to call, "OMG Your Talents." I challenge you to:

- **OWN your talents.** Write down at the end of each day every activity you did that energized you and all the activities that drained you. Pay special attention to how your body reacted and the sensations you had as you did those activities.

- **MASTER your talents.** If you already know and have explored your strengths, research ways to get even better at them. Take a class, engage a coach, or mentor.

- **GIVE AWAY your talents.** Find opportunities in your home, at work, or in your community to contribute your talents to another person, a group, or an organization.

For more helpful tips, try these additional resources:

- Strengthsfinder 2.0 by Tom Rath
- "Trombone Player Wanted" by Marcus Buckingham
- Listen to my Time to Come Alive podcast, especially the "O.M.G. Your Talents" episode
  - **YouTube:** *https://youtu.be/E09HiJw7h5s*
  - **Spotify:** *https://open.spotify.com/ episode/6ANIXvJLFBVDRTWSSJ44yv*

BIOGRAPHY

Being a curious and creative learner has set Valerie apart as a leadership coach and professional speaker. Her winning combination is engaging individuals and groups to discover, develop, and contribute their talents to the planet.

For more than twenty years, her career path included the international leadership program, Up With People, the Dallas Regional Chamber of Commerce, and the Hyatt Hotels and Resorts Corporation.

In 2018, she established her company, Connect to Joy, LLC. Her thought-provoking questions and unique strategies empower people from all walks of life. Her group workshops and one-on-one sessions are designed to go beyond concepts and data points, to shine a light on what has heart and meaning.

As a world-traveler, Valerie has developed and transformed leaders throughout Latin America, North America, and Europe to become more conscious, connected, and creative.

She received her executive coaching certification from University of California at Berkeley, where she serves as an assistant professor. She holds a B.A. in Public Relations and Spanish from the University of Alabama.

Valerie is a native Spanish-speaker from the Republic of Panama. She loves Latin dancing, playing tennis, and she claims Dallas as her home and has the cowboy boots to prove it!

Valerie Hope

Leadership Coach & Professional Speaker

Years in HR: 20

Valerie@valeriehope.com

214-507-2983 / www.ValerieHope.com

BY NAYSA APARICIO-HERNANDEZ

"Following our dreams is how we can do more and do it even better."

This is probably the hardest thing I have ever done in my life. When Priscilla asked me to write my story for this book, I froze. Wait, what? My story? What do you mean by write my story? I can write a policy or a termination letter, but my story? In English? You've got to be kidding me!

But here I am, and I am very honored to do it. I grabbed all my feelings and emotions and started writing. My name is Naysa Aparicio-Hernandez, and this is my story.

STEPPING INTO HR

I came to the U.S. exactly twenty years ago with my

husband and our six-year-old son. I had a great life in Venezuela. My family was what you would call a middle-class family. We did not have much money, but enough to live. This meant we could not travel or afford luxuries; but it was enough to have a good life filled with memories that my parents created. I was the only girl of four siblings.

All my brothers went to public schools and graduated from public universities because my parents didn't have the money to pay for a private university. When it was my turn to go to college, I knew I wanted to study human resources. I have known this since I was seventeen years old. I have always been there for others, listened to them, and helped them if possible. But unfortunately, the only university in Venezuela that offered a human resources program was a private university.

I applied for a full scholarship and among thousands of students, I received it due to my excellent grades. The scholarship was conditional and required I maintain an above average GPA for all five years. Not as easy-peasy as I thought. But I was able to do it, and at the end of those five years I was married and had a two-year-old toddler.

With my new degree, I found a job as an HR Assistant in the second biggest manufacturing company of air filters for gas oil turbines. Venezuela remains one of the top ten oil-producing countries in the world. In two years, I was promoted to HR Manager and after two more years, I finally decided to move on and accept another position in an advertising company. Everything was good.

I was barely one month into my new job when my husband received a job offer with a company in Chicago. I took one look at his face and knew he wanted to accept it. I had to support him, but I didn't even know where Chicago was on the map!

We landed in Chicago on a Saturday in July 2000. My husband started his new job the following Monday. That summer was like a vacation. Chicago is beautiful, and I enjoyed visiting museums and the beaches with my son.

Then fall came. School started and I found myself alone at home with no friends, no English, and no job. I started missing my parents and my life in Venezuela. Everything, from the language to the food, was strange and different. I felt so lost that I cried every day for six months. I was so miserable.

I needed to pull myself together for the sake of my son and my marriage. I start sending resumes, but no one would call me, not even for an interview. Some friends told me that without a work history in the U.S., I would never be able to land a job, especially in HR. They recommended that I change careers, but the only good options I had were babysitting and working in retail. Even then, they told me to take my degree out of my resume and instead pretend that I didn't have any education or experience at all. That was unacceptable to me. I have sacrificed a lot for my degree and a career that I loved, so in the end I decided I wanted to stay in HR, whatever that meant.

FORGING AHEAD

I started to study English at the College of DuPage and hung out with English speakers, mostly neighbors that had kids the same age as my son. They helped me a lot. I also started taking HR courses in English which helped me to understand the concepts and definitions of HR in this country. Despite my efforts, time passed, and I still had no job.

After three years, we welcomed a daughter. With a baby at home, I had to put my return to work aside for a while, even though money was tighter than ever. My husband started working two jobs in order to make ends meet.

While I was at home, I embraced my creativity. I took evening classes and graduated as a professional cake decorator, receiving an offer to be a cake decorating instructor. It paid twenty-five dollars an hour! Those classes were lifesavers because I was earning some money while practicing my English in front of twenty English-speaking students. They were learning from me, but they didn't know that I was also learning from them. I taught cake decorating for three years.

Then, in 2006, six years after I landed in Chicago, I finally found a job as a recruiter for the Hispanic market of a well-known direct sales company. Coming back to my field gave me the strength I needed. After three months, I found a job as an HR Assistant at a 3PL (Third Party Logistics company), which paid me a little bit more. My husband finally was able to quit his second job. After only six months, I was promoted to HR Generalist.

The logistics industry turned out to be a challenge. With men dominating the scene, I found myself faced with many disadvantages: I was a woman, Hispanic, and an immigrant. I had to work harder than anyone else to show my value and what I could bring to the business. It got even harder when tragedy struck six months later.

POWER OF POSITIVITY

It was Tuesday morning, payroll day. I was approving all timecards and processing the payroll that was due at nine o'clock in the morning in order to meet the deadline. I had a candidate for the HR assistant position waiting for me in the lobby to start that same day. The HR Manager and the Director of Operations were waiting for some reports they had asked me to run that morning. Suddenly, I was unable to see through my left eye. Within minutes, the left side of my face became numb, and then my left arm. I panicked. My dad had suffered a stroke the year before and became bedridden. He could not move or talk anymore. Was I having a stroke as well? I barely got to the Director of Operations' office. He looked at me and said, "We're taking you to the ER."

The following two weeks are still a blur to me. After several blood tests, MRIs, and a spinal tap, the results were devastating. I was diagnosed with Multiple Sclerosis (MS), an autoimmune, disabling disease of the brain and spinal cord. The doctor told me that with the number of lesions I had, the probability of being in a wheelchair in four years was extremely high. I was in my early thirties and my youngest child was just three years old. I had just started to gain experience in the field I loved. How could this happen? Why did it happen to me?

The more I learned about my new condition, the more depressed I became. Several factors were believed to trigger the symptoms: stress, heat, and even supplements. The treatments were very invasive, and the side effects were even worse. The doctors recommended that I resign from my job to avoid stress. I did not want to do that; another option had to exist.

My husband and I sat down one night after the kids were sleeping. I was crying inconsolably. He asked me, "Naysa, what do you want to do? Stop listening to what everybody else is telling you what you should do, and just think about what your heart is telling you to do." In that very moment, I decided what I did and didn't want. I wanted to be there for my kids and my husband. I wanted to be the successful HR professional I had always dreamed of becoming. I did not want this condition to take over my life. I had so many things to see: my kids' graduations, their weddings, their children. There were so many accomplishments to achieve, so much life I still wanted to live to the fullest.

That was it. I started my treatment and after three years, I was promoted to HR manager. The following year, the company made me senior HR manager with three U.S. locations. I led the HR functions for those facilities, ensuring that all departmental needs were being met and I supported key leaders in solving business and human resources issues.

After eight years working for that company, I moved on and worked for an international IT consulting company headquartered in India, where I was exposed to global HR. I was more focused in talent management initiatives such as performance management, promotions, and competency development. With more than five thousand employees across the U.S., I traveled to several states and met wonderful people on that journey.

When travelling started to take a toll on me, I decided to look for a local job and took a position as an HR Manager position at a manufacturing company overseeing three buildings, with two in Illinois and one in Ohio. This job gave me the opportunity to recharge. I studied for six months to take the Senior Professional in Human Resource Management certification, which I passed. After this, I found a Human Resources Director position for a logistics, warehousing, and transportation group. After two years, they promoted me to Vice President of Human Resources. I still worked in a male-dominated industry, and for a while I was the only female on the executive team; while I remain the only Hispanic person on the team to this day, I am honored to have a great group that reports to me and sees me as their role model.

But none of this was easy. I have had hard times. I have done three chemotherapies in 13 years to control some of the bad symptoms. The treatments I have had were very invasive. It took me a long time to find a treatment that works for me. More than once, I had to sit and reprogram myself, so I wouldn't forget that I've got this. My condition has never defined who I am. My doctor still looks at me and wonders how I am walking. She believes it is because of my attitude and the way I confront adversity. I believe it is not only that, but also the desire to follow my dreams. It can work for anyone. Following our dreams is how we can do more and do it even better. You don't have to rush to be successful; take all the time you need. Just be persistent and find what works for you.

REFLECT AND RISE

One person told me once, you won't know if you are on the right track if you don't know where you are going. If my goal was to be a rocket science engineer, I would've definitely been on the wrong track. Sit and think about where you want to be in one, three, five years; not only in your profession and career, but also in your personal and health life. Take the actions needed to change your future now. Are you doing everything in your reach to achieve your goals? Do you have a clear vision of where or what you want to be?

I challenge you to write down three columns. Separate your dreams in one, three, and five years from now. Try to be realistic, but don't hold yourself to them. Start writing down your goals at short term. Do you want to lose ten pounds? Would you prefer to have a different job or work in a different industry? After that, move on to your midterm and long-term goals. You will be amazed when you start crossing off everything on your list!

BIOGRAPHY

Naysa Aparicio-Hernandez is currently the Vice President of Human Resources at RJW Logistics Group, where she directs the successful administration of the HR function, company's staffing goals and strategies to support productive and profitable business operations.

Naysa has more than 20 years of experience in Human Resources and has worked in many different industries including logistics, manufacturing, transportation, warehousing and IT. She holds a bachelor's degree in Industrial Relations from the Universidad Católica Andres Bello in Venezuela and is certified as Senior Professional in Human Resources Management (SPHR) by the Human Resources Certification Institute (HRCI) in the U.S. Naysa has earned several awards during her career from Special HR Initiative to Employee of the Year. She speaks English, Spanish and Italian. In addition, she has been an activist for the National Multiple Sclerosis Society since 2009.

When she is not in strategic planning meetings, Naysa enjoys baking and traveling with her husband and kids.

Naysa Aparicio-Hernandez

VP of HR

Years in HR: 20

naysa@hotmail.com

LinkedIn.com/in/napariciohernandez

FINDING HR

BY KATIE LOPES

"Network and practice your public speaking skills."

Do you remember your response the first time your teacher asked what you wanted to be when you grew up? I don't. Oftentimes I would copy someone else's answer of becoming a doctor, teacher, or veterinarian, not realizing it was up to my imagination to dream big about my future. However, I do remember the time I shared my answer publicly for the fourth-grade book project that was distributed to our parents—and the look of shock my mother had upon reading my submission. My proud contribution read: "When I grow up, I want to work at Target just like my mom. She works hard and is happy."

It was confusing to explain to my mom that I admired her so much that I wanted to be just like her, only to learn that my mom wanted me to do anything else but follow in her footsteps. I didn't understand. All of the brown women in my life worked hard in jobs that supported their families. My mom gloated about the group benefits she received at Target, my aunts would clean beautiful mansions in the Malibu hills, and my grandma still cooked and cleaned for her same employer in Beverly Hills after more than fifteen years. Weren't their jobs examples of my future destiny?

FAMILY AND FREEDOM

That submission must have triggered something in *mami* because from then on she focused our conversations on the value of education and how it was the key to achieving success in America. *Mami* immigrated from Guatemala when she was sixteen, and although she didn't speak English, she started working at a garment factory while cleaning houses on the side with her sisters. A decade later, she obtained her permanent resident card and was finally able to work for corporations in entry-level positions. *Mami* started sharing the details of her past jobs to illustrate the struggle she experienced to survive in America, with no formal education, language barriers, and limitations of citizenship status. My mom understood that U.S. citizenship could provide her better opportunities, so she put in the work to take ESL classes to improve her English and embraced technology as it became more evident in the workplace. In many ways, her struggles influenced the development of my work ethic.

Mami would work five days straight at her full-time job, clean an average of three homes during the week, and still find time to fill out work paperwork with my help as I translated them for her. She shared her experiences and frustrations to emphasize the message: get a higher education to work smarter, not harder. But deciding what career to choose was always my conundrum.

When I graduated high school, I decided I needed to move away from the safety blanket of Los Angeles to try new opportunities. I packed two suitcases and made my way to San Francisco State University (SFSU) on a four-year, sponsored scholarship, with an undeclared major. My mother and brother flew with me to drop me off and move me into my on-campus apartment the day before orientation. It was a surreal experience checking-in at the desk with the RA. I assured them I didn't need a dolly to unload a car full of dorm room swag like others in line; I had everything I needed in my suitcases.

The three of us walked to my apartment, where my brother helped me claim the bed nearest to the window and my mom helped me unpack my clothes. After my roommate arrived and her parents met my mom, my family of three hugged goodbye. That first night I bought a box of cereal and milk to celebrate my independence and cried myself to sleep. No one in my family had ever gone to college. This was all new territory, and it felt extremely lonely.

The first year was tough as I was adjusting to life away from family. I experienced Imposter Syndrome as I struggled to comprehend class readings and had to work full-time at a local retail shop to make ends meet since my scholarship only covered tuition costs. I made it through the first year with the support of the Latina sorority I joined, *Sigma Pi Alpha*, where I met other first-generation Latinas who were breaking barriers in their families as well. They held me accountable to my study hours, encouraged me to maintain a high GPA, and to be involved in the community through philanthropy work. Many conversations were had in that support group about what careers we dreamed about as we pursued higher education. Many of my *hermanas* knew they wanted to study social work, child adolescent development, or biology research, yet I couldn't make up my mind. For the next four years, I gravitated towards classes centered in anthropology and ethnic studies, which eventually earned me enough credits to graduate with a BA in Anthropology by the Spring of 2011.

So there I was, four years after moving away from home, with a college diploma in hand, thirty-thousand dollars in debt, with still no idea what career I wanted.

I wasn't ready to admit my non-existent career plans to my family, but I stayed in San Francisco living in cheap housing situations while working three jobs to make ends meet. I worked at a small bakery at four o'clock in the morning through the morning rush hour, ran to the skincare retail job that started at eleven, and dragged myself to another beauty shop at four in the afternoon to close the boutique at eight. Rest and repeat.

I applied anywhere and everywhere for an entry-level opportunity but couldn't get any call backs. I finally reached out to a sorority sister who worked at a bank and asked if she could put in a good word for me to the branch manager of the location where I had recently applied. The power of networking not only got me the interview, but she vouched for me when the managers were reviewing my application and were unsure if they should hire a recent college graduate with no experience or desire to work in the financial industry.

FINDING MY WAY

Thanks to that connection, I built a promising career path in the first couple of years and a reputation of audit accuracy, mad organization skills, and proficient bilingual skills to close sales. I was quickly sought after by other managers, and was promoted to a banker position and relocated to a struggling branch in The Mission, a predominantly Latino neighborhood, to help the manager focus on diversifying the access of services to the community.

I was sent to a week-long banker training program to learn how to become a better salesperson, which is where I met a fantastic company trainer by the name of Michelle. I was in awe of how she built training curriculums, how she could engage different personalities in the room, and provide resources to help us develop in our respective roles. Most of all, I was surprised to see in a corporation, for the first time, a Latina in a higher-level position, not just an entry-level job. I asked Michelle to chat with me one day over lunch so she could share her career path with me, and that's how I discovered the Learning and Development (L&D) focus of human resources. Michelle talked about how she pursued the HR field, but her curiosity for educating others influenced her to pursue a career in L&D. I asked for tips on how to build skills for an eventual position in HR, and to this day they were the best pieces of advice I ever received: (1) start networking, and (2) practice your public speaking skills.

I worked in the financial industry for a couple of more years before switching to the insurance industry, still in a sales-related role. It was difficult attempting to get my foot into HR without the formal education background, but I focused on practicing the advice Michelle gave me. I substituted for my boss at her BNI networking groups on Tuesdays at seven o'clock in the morning, and volunteered for opportunities to speak to communities so I could practice my public speaking skills. I stumbled through awkward conversations, confronted stage fright, and eventually practiced these skills long enough that it became second nature for me to walk into a room and strike up a professional conversation with the person next to me in line.

Collectively, I worked in the financial and insurance sector for eight years. I spoke with clients who were struggling to make ends meet, others who were creating a protection plan for their family's legacy, and folks who were building a six-figure business from their homes. These experiences opened my eyes to the inequalities that existed in these industries. I could hear the bias in commentary from coworkers who didn't know how to speak to clients with different values or beliefs. These same coworkers would turn around and make fun of me for having tolerance to accept reading material from Jehovah's Witnesses, or roll their eyes if I enunciated a client's name as they taught me to pronounce it. There was so much that I observed and yet couldn't find the words to describe the microaggressions I witnessed. I kept wondering how I could influence or address these concerns in the workplace and grew more curious about what a career in HR could look like for me.

OPPORTUNITY IN CHICAGO

In 2015, I moved to Chicago with my partner, where

we decided to start a new chapter in a more affordable city. One of the many reasons I chose Chicago was for access to the various universities in the area, where I planned to apply for an HR degree. I eventually got accepted into Northwestern University for a post-baccalaureate certificate program (think of it like a minor for my BA) in the fundamentals of HR. For the next year and a half, I coordinated full-time work, part-time school, while juggling my relationship in my few free moments. From the moment I sat in my first HR class called "Conflict Resolution," I knew I was destined to work in HR. I loved all of the readings, analyzing the importance and role of HR in an organization, and for the first time I *dreamed* about building my career into an HR Director role.

I timed the near end of my program with my intensive application process into an entry-level HR job. I took the leap from making good money to making minimum wage as a recruiting coordinator on a contract basis. I tried hard not to focus on the fact that it felt like a step back, so I continued to complete my courses while applying for all the job opportunities I could find. I even created a spreadsheet to help me track the status of more than two hundred applications I submitted.

One day, I decided to reach out to a recruiter that direct messaged me on LinkedIn and had an honest conversation about what I was seeking. I was an experienced working professional looking for an opportunity to step into an HR role where I could be mentored by a leader in a small to mid-sized business, influence the changes of the department, and feel I am making a difference by supporting the workers of the organization with my bilingual skills. It felt like the universe listened to me because next thing I knew I had an interview for an HR coordinator role in a manufacturing organization where I could work alongside the director of HR. I had a two-hour long interview, we talked about my courses, my experience in previous jobs, and my goals for a career in HR. I left feeling great about it all and my gut was giving me that happy funny feeling. Then I got a call back at the end of the week; they moved forward with another candidate.

The loss of the opportunity was a bit of a blow, but I decided to take my mind off it and prepare for my friend's wedding in Napa. I was at the airport waiting for boarding to start when I received a call from the recruiter. The other candidate accepted a different job offer and I was the runner up for the position, so they wanted to make me an offer if I was still interested. I listened to the details of the offer and the package and decided to negotiate for fifteen percent more than what they initially offered. I outlined the struggle they had in recruiting a bilingual professional who was willing to travel to the company's location. I was not intimidated to do so, and in fact I had years of assisting in translations of conversations and documents. The commute was no problem as long as they understood that part of the increase I was asking for was not only for my experienced skillset but also to cover the increase in my transportation costs. By the time I landed in California five hours later, I had received the counteroffer with the increased salary I requested. I happily signed the offer letter and enjoyed the break in Napa before returning to Chicago to begin my new career opportunity.

It's been two years since I've started working in HR, and every month I feel more confident in my stride. All of the experience I built working in the financial and insurance industries helped me understand the administrative and negotiation aspects that happen on the HR side. I've proven to be a quick learner and have taken over many of the administrative functions of the HR role. I'm also included in business strategy conversations with the support of my director. There are many challenges I face, particularly learning business Spanish for topics I have no idea how to translate (i.e. phishing scams, I still don't know the translation). I'm climbing up the HR career ladder in the manufacturing industry, in an organization where HR already has its seat at the table. For the first time since I shared my future career for that class book project, I can confidently say I will be a groundbreaking Latina HR leader when I grow up.

I often talk to my mom on a weekly basis with updates about my job. I'll ask for her assistance in translating phrases that I struggle with, and I share the challenges I face with employee relation issues. *Mami* is a good listener; she knows just what to say to make me feel confident in my decisions. She's proud of what I've done thus far, for achieving new levels she could never dream of. I tell her it's not that she didn't achieve these successes herself; in fact, she taught me how to treat people with respect, to be an active listener, to think logically before responding emotionally, and that an act of kindness builds trust in the most stubborn relationships. She taught me all of these life lessons and they have built me into the woman I am today. Thanks to her, my momentum has just begun.

REFLECT AND RISE

One of my earliest pieces of advice was to network. Here are some answers to networking FAQs.

Find events that focus on a topic of interest, either in-person or virtual. Have a notepad handy to jot down the names of people you meet that you'd like to get to know better. Look them up via LinkedIn, send a personalized note referencing where you met, and invite them for a 1-1 virtual coffee.

What questions should I ask when networking?

Do some research before your 1-1 meeting. Look at their LinkedIn profile to understand their current position, and where they've worked before. Create questions about their current role, ask about their experience in a program, and also ask if they recommend any local resources for your professional development either in HR or in your industry.

How do I practice my public speaking skills?

Record yourself reading a script. Listen for any "filler words" to identify areas of your speech that you're uncomfortable with; then challenge yourself to read through a script without filler words. Extra points if you do a video recording! Look at your facial expressions. Where can you take deep breaths to appear more relaxed and confident?

BIOGRAPHY

Katie Lopes started her HR career in 2018 as a recruiting coordinator and quickly moved into an HR generalist role. Currently, she works in the manufacturing industry where her responsibilities range from benefits and leave administration, overseeing payroll, leading investigations for employee relations, and serving as an HR business partner to management. As a bilingual Latina, she constantly navigates conversations in multilingual workplaces with a lens of cultural and emotional awareness.

Katie is a Californian native, now living in the Midwest. She obtained her B.A. in Anthropology from San Francisco State University, and a post-baccalaureate certificate in Fundamentals of HR from Northwestern University. She is the founder of "Latina in HR," a personal blog to share her stories of breaking into human resources. When she's not working or blogging, you can find her hiking local trails or biking around town.

Katie Lopes

HR Anthropologist

Years in HR: 2

info@latinainhr.com

Instagram: @LatinainHR

BY MYRIAM DEL ANGEL

"If you make a good impression, people will remember you and think of you for potential roles."

Growing up in a predominantly Mexican, Chicago neighborhood called Little Village, I was not exposed to various types of careers. Both my parents owned businesses. My mom owned a hair salon and my dad was a mechanic. In my household, the goal after high school was to get a job. Going to college was considered unnecessary. My dad would say, *"¿Vas a gastar dinero en la universidad en lugar de ganar dinero? ¿Estas loca?"* (You are going to spend money on college instead of making money?! Are you crazy?!") Thankfully, I had a circle of friends who were preparing to apply to college and helped me through the process.

INTRO TO HR

After being accepted to the University of Illinois at

Chicago (UIC), I started to get into the groove of college life. Unfortunately, it was very difficult for my parents to understand late night study sessions, etc. so it was obvious that it would be best for everyone if I moved into the dorms. It was such a great experience, meeting people from all over the world and learning about different cultures and personalities. By sophomore year, I decided to apply to become a Resident Advisor (RA). As an RA, your job is to work with other RAs and with hall residents to facilitate an environment within the dorms that contributes to the overall mental, social, physical, moral, and cultural growth of the students. The RA helps students understand the policies of the college and represents the needs of students to the administration. Unknowingly, this was my first exposure to human resources!

Being an RA helped out a bit financially, but like most struggling college students, I had to get a part-time job to help with tuition and expenses. I worked as a waitress, barista, hotel front desk agent, parking garage attendant, and student worker (working in various departments throughout the university). During one of my student employment positions, I worked for the Latin American Recruitment and Educational Services Program (LARES). It was a program that was geared toward Latinx students and provided academic support and guidance throughout their college years. Within this role I was exposed to many types of careers paths.

I really did not know what I wanted to study. I switched my major, like many college students do, from liberal arts to business, to computer science, to psychology, etc. During one of my conversations with a student career counselor, he asked me "What do you see yourself doing after college?" I had no clue! "What are your interests?" I like working with people. "What are your skills?" I can communicate effectively, I am a good listener, and I genuinely like people. "Have you ever heard of human resources?" Um, no! The university did not have a human resources curriculum, so it was the first time I had ever heard of this career path. He recommended that I do some research and talk to different individuals in that field. He shared a list of contacts and suggested if I was truly interested in pursuing this field, I should consider transferring to Northeastern Illinois University (NEIU), which offered an undergraduate and graduate program in HR. It also had lower tuition.

NETWORKING IN ACTION

After having a few meetings with HR professionals, I decided to apply to NEIU. I took classes like adult learning, instructional technique, and dynamics of working with people. I realized I really enjoyed what I was learning. I worked full time and went to school on a part-time basis. Though it would take me eight years, I would be the first one in my family to receive a college education.

After graduation, I started working as a training coordinator, scheduling required training for employees. I was an underrepresented minority on my team and within the organization. That was definitely an eye opener, and I had to learn how to navigate my career not only being new in HR, but also within the culture, or lack thereof, of the organization. I learned that the more people I knew within the organization, the more opportunities I had for growth. If you make a good impression, people will remember you and think of you for potential roles.

I started to attend various networking events, beginning with diversity-focused ones, but then began attending any which showcased my passion and interests. At one networking event, I met a Microsoft recruiter who submitted my resume for a recruiter role in their corporate offices in Redmond, Washington. It was a great experience to fly there and interview. Unfortunately, I did not get an offer. Then, six months later, she reached out to me about a potential recruiting role in their Chicago office. I must have made such a good impression because she remembered me and thought of me for the new role. I interviewed and received an offer within two weeks.

After a few years at Microsoft, I decided it was time for me to diversify my HR skills. I went from being a compensation consultant at the University of Chicago to a diversity campus recruiter for Accenture. I traveled extensively in the U.S. and Puerto Rico, searching for females and people of color to join their technology groups.

Then life happened. I had my first child and could no longer travel. I networked again and found a role within Accenture as an HR Representative, working from home, full time. As an HR representative, I was responsible for ensuring that the companies' policies and programs were implemented and was a resource for the employees I supported. I had two more children, and then, during my third pregnancy, I was laid off. The company decided to outsource their HR services to South America. I was devastated but enjoyed my time off with my children. When I was ready to go back to work, I tapped into my network and landed a role within Deloitte as an HR Manager. This role combined my recruiting and HR rep skills. I was responsible for not only supporting a group in HR matters, but also staffing projects.

A year later, a former colleague at another organization reached out to me about a potential role within Ernst & Young (EY). I jumped at this new opportunity. At EY, my responsibility grew from HR support and staffing to assisting in the diversity efforts within the organization. I had the opportunity to lead these efforts, specifically around female representation in the executive space. During this time balancing family and work life was a big challenge.

Having three kids under six years old had me reevaluate my priorities and I wanted to find a role where there was no travel and a regular work schedule. I applied for a part-time opportunity at UIC's College of Business. The dean needed help in building corporate relationships, and because of my diverse experience and growing network, I was offered a full-time opportunity as the director of corporate engagement in their newly-formed career center. I was tasked in leading a team and building a strategy around student outreach, employer relations, and diversity retention.

This role took my networking skills to the next level. I had to go out and convince employers to recruit at the university. It was very fulfilling to help navigate college students through their career journey. After a few years, my team and I successfully grew the career center and I felt it was time for me to return to the HR world.

A NEW DIRECTION

Through my contacts from UIC, I was presented with an HR opportunity at PricewaterhouseCoopers (PwC) in their Los Angeles office. It was a great experience to live in California, but after a year, I decided to transfer back to the PwC Chicago office, where I currently work. I've gone from being an HR business partner to now working on the Flex team. This team is a group of highly experienced

HR individuals who cover anyone in any HR function (HR, recruiting, strategy, diversity, staffing, etc.) across all lines of services in the United States, when they are out on leave. I can be on a strategy project for a few months or an HR project for a year or more. All my past experiences and skills have led me into the role of HR consultant, which I truly enjoy. HR is a very rewarding career because you can help develop the people around you and really make a difference in someone's career journey.

From my story, I hope you realize that networking is important to your success throughout every stage of your career. When you invest in your professional relationships, it can keep you up to date on the job market, help you meet potential mentors, and obtain information on resources and tools that will help you in your career. If you are uncomfortable with networking, you can google tips on networking and practice with your friends and family. Also, join organizations such as Society of Human Resources Management (https://shrm.org/) or those that share your passion and goals.

REFLECT AND RISE

Here are some tips to help you network:

- **Look at your current network.** Is it complete?
- **Reach out to people in your network with specific goals in mind.** This can be an invitation to

meet individually, to get a referral, or to ask for a professional opinion.

- **If possible, meet in person, or on a Zoom call.**
- **Be yourself.** Authenticity is key to being able to help each other.
- **Share your goals and interests.** Don't forget your hobbies and other possible things in common.
- **Ask specific questions.** Make the most of your networking time.
- **Listen more than you speak.** Discover how you can help the person you are networking with.
- **Thank them and follow up.** Make a good last impression.
- **Keep in touch.**

BIOGRAPHY

Myriam Del Angel is Colombian/Mexican and was born and raised in Chicago. She holds a bachelor's degree in human resources development from Northeastern Illinois University. She is a visionary, results-oriented human resources leader with more than twenty years of experience in performance management, resource management, compensation, talent acquisition, employee relations, strategy and diversity, equity, and inclusion (DEI). She has worked at various organizations such as Arthur Andersen,

Microsoft, Accenture, University of Chicago, Deloitte, Ernst & Young, the University of Illinois at Chicago (UIC), and PricewaterhouseCoopers (PwC). She currently lives near downtown Chicago with her three kids, Laila, Mia, and Luca. She enjoys yoga, running, traveling, bartending, and Latin dancing.

Myriam Del Angel

HR Manager

Years in HR: 20

myriamdelangelmiranda@gmail.com

Linkedin.com: /in/mdmiranda/

BY MONICA TIJERINA

"There is value in creating opportunities in places others might not."

My story is not entirely mine, and it doesn't fit neatly into a box. I am all that I am because of my mom – my immigrant, physically disabled, uneducated, single, relentlessly optimistic mom. My story is an extension of hers and my place in the world is built on her understanding and insistence that if the world doesn't have a bright, sunny box filled with opportunity for you, make one.

I work for one of the most recognizable brands in the world in the field of Corporate Social Responsibility (CSR). CSR sits in the intersection of everything a business does and the people and communities it affects. Because of my early experiences and the ever-present influence and support of my mom, I thrive in the spaces where these intersections occur. I see connections and create opportunities in places others don't.

MOM AND ME

My mom came to the United States from Colombia in her twenties. She met my dad in southwest Texas, where I was born, and spoke only Spanish for the first few years of my life. When I was about three years old, my parents split up and my mom and I moved to northern Michigan to be near her sister; her only other relative in the U.S. If you can't picture northern Michigan as a "hub" of ethnic and cultural diversity waiting to welcome us now, imagine it forty years ago.

On paper, we were a formula for disaster. My mom had recently been diagnosed with a giant brain aneurysm (that's the actual medical diagnosis) and seizure disorder, she spoke no English, she had less than a high school education, and she was now a single mom. But my mom was no ordinary human. She always looked past the barriers and saw possibilities around every corner – especially for me.

In Michigan, my mom struggled to learn English. I was young, and learning a new language came more easily to me. I helped my mom navigate our new home, medical appointments, a new baby sister, and a new language. In turn, she filled my head with the idea that I was the smartest child that ever lived, capable of accomplishing anything I wanted. My mom didn't know a lot about the career options available to the smartest child that ever lived, but as a person who had been in and out of many hospitals, she knew doctors were smart, they were respected, and made a lot more money than she did. I trusted her plan for my future and set my sights on becoming a doctor.

Because of her medical diagnosis, my mom could not get a job, so she invested everything she had into giving my sister and me a happy childhood and setting us up for future success. In third grade, my mom secured scholarships to a private Catholic school for us. I still don't know how she did it, but every year my mom would find a ride from someone, because we couldn't afford a car, walk into the school and in broken English, convince the administrators to let her daughters attend for free.

Later in life, my mom shared that while a solid religious foundation was great, what she really wanted was for us to be surrounded by people who were more affluent than us so we would set our future plans and expectations as they did. She wanted to make sure that even though we lived in public housing, we knew the world and the people outside of our building. While the kids in my neighborhood were content with barely graduating high school, the kids at my school were all expected to go to college. My experience was defined by one foot in a highly affluent environment and the other in our public housing complex. Although I didn't fit neatly in either, I created my own space navigating both million-dollar mansions and the smoke-filled hallways of our apartment building with ease.

Her theory about private school was right. There was so much we didn't know that those around me did. I didn't know that the ACT test was important and only showed up on time because my best friend told me she'd be mad at me if I didn't. I applied to the University of Michigan because it's where my mom had recovered from brain surgery, and she said, "The kids there seemed to have so much fun." I didn't apply to any other schools because I didn't understand that they had the option to deny me. I also didn't know that I was seen as anything more than my abilities until my high school classmate started complaining that the only reason I got into that university, and she didn't, was because I was a minority. My mom assured me that she was just jealous because I was the smartest child that ever lived.

FINDING MY TRIBE

Going into college, I was uniquely armed with the experiences and network of a private school, coupled with a whole lot of hustle and grit. Despite how well prepared I thought I was, the transition to college was tough. In addition to the challenging academics, I was working part-time, ill-prepared to manage my own finances, and I continued to play an important role in the well-being of my mom and sister, who were now four hours away.

While I eventually figured out how to manage college, I didn't thrive until I began finding the other students like me. I tried to connect with other former private school students, but I wasn't fancy enough. I tried the Latino student organization, but I spoke and dressed wrong, and wasn't "Latino" enough. Eventually, I found the other students like me who, in their own ways, had each been navigating different spaces too. When we found each other, we held on tight and created our own secret society, in a sense, of people charting new paths informed by disparate experiences. We spent countless hours comparing experiences, learning from each other, and creating an inviting space for others like us.

As young people do in college, I was learning more about the world and my place in it. I had a heavy pre-med course load but my passion laid elsewhere. A few years in, I knew I didn't have a passion for medicine like I did for social justice. I completed my bachelor of science degree but I wasn't headed to medical school. I signed up for a two-year assignment in Americorps to serve under-resourced communities in Chicago.

Two weeks into my Americorps assignment, my mom got really sick and I had to drop out to head home and be with her. When I arrived, she was determined to get better as quickly as possible so I could get back to making a life for myself. I swear, she practically kicked me out.

After my mom healed, I moved to Washington, DC with a friend, somewhat on a whim. It was not exactly the post-college planning process I'd imagined, but after two years in

Washington, DC, I knew it was time to go back to school for a master's degree and I was clear on what I wanted to study. Unlike undergrad, this time I was firmly on my own path, a path my mom didn't completely understand, but supported completely. I returned to the University of Michigan to complete a master's degree in public policy with a focus on social welfare policy.

WORK AND SERVICE

Immediately after graduate school, a classmate helped me secure a job in local government working with social service providers across the county. I blossomed in that role. As a person who had once been on the receiving end of various social services from housing and food assistance to public health and social worker services, this was a world I really understood. I saw my family in the faces of the people we were helping. I could relate to the physical and emotional needs and the experiences of individuals and families receiving these services. My early life experiences, coupled with my education, allowed me to create a space where I could analytically, yet compassionately identify, evaluate, and lobby for solutions.

In my work with the county social service providers, we identified an opportunity to work better with private funders to target resources and address the most pressing needs of people in the community. We created a series of conversations with social service agencies and private funders to identify how we could deliver on the goals of each while delivering on the shared goal of creating a vibrant community where everyone could thrive. Through these conversations, I saw that someone like me could do a lot of good within a corporation, and I met a woman at Pfizer who agreed.

At Pfizer, everyone I worked with was highly educated and represented some of the world's most respected pharmaceutical scientists. It was a pretty intimidating place. However, because of my experiences and education, I was able to communicate the needs of the community to the scientists and corporate leaders who may or may not have experienced those needs firsthand. Conversely, I could communicate the value of the lifesaving, scientific work done by the professionals at Pfizer to community members who had never stepped inside a pharmaceutical laboratory. As a young person, I could never have imagined that this kind of work existed. It was, and is, a really unique opportunity, and I was perfect for it.

My mom always told me, "*Mami*, don't think about getting married until you're at least thirty, you have a career, and you own a home." Right on schedule, I met Mark, a scientist at Pfizer, a few weeks before my thirtieth birthday. Mark is different than me in more ways than I can count but true to form, the intersection of our shared values and passion for life make him my perfect complement. At Pfizer, I discovered corporate social responsibility and my husband

Mark. I've been hooked on both ever since.

After Mark and I got married, we moved to Chicago. I began searching for corporate social responsibility jobs and was not having any luck in this niche profession. So, with a little hustle and lot of networking, I landed a job in global marketing at McDonald's. I had zero marketing experience but my unique blend of experiences was just what they were looking for. In that role, I managed a council of global scientific experts as well as a council of "average" parents to inform our business.

I've had a number of roles at McDonald's, in marketing, community engagement, diversity & inclusion and currently in global HR strategy. Each role has allowed me to influence how the company can do business in a way that creates shared value. Currently, I'm leading a global program focused on giving youth access to training that can help them connect with work and education, and I lead the McDonald's headquarters chapter of the Hispanic Employee Business Network. I've been able to carve out roles for myself because the company sees that there is value in creating opportunities in places others might not... like at the intersection of what our business does and the communities it affects.

REFLECT AND RISE

My challenge to other Latinas is to be like my mom. And here are some of the things she taught me that I hope you can incorporate into your own life.

1. **Be relentlessly optimistic about your potential.**
   The world can make you look at your differences as
   weaknesses, but they can actually be the things that
   allow you to succeed in places and in ways others
   can't.

2. **Be confident in the value you bring.** If you don't
   see a professional role that can leverage that value
   – create it.

3. **Never forget that our stories are all intertwined.**
   My mom knew that her story would not be complete
   until she ensured my sister and I would find success
   in life. Remember that your story isn't complete until
   you've done all you can to elevate the women who
   come after you.

BIOGRAPHY

Monica Tijerina joined McDonald's global marketing
team in 2012 and currently serves as the director of Global
People Strategy, overseeing McDonald's Global Youth
Opportunity Program and Global Employee Volunteer
Strategy. She helps deliver on McDonald's Scale for Good
commitment to reduce barriers to employment for two million
young people as well as harness the passion of employee
volunteers to give back to McDonald's communities.

Prior to joining McDonald's, Monica worked in corporate responsibility and reputation for Pfizer, Inc. where she managed local and global philanthropic and volunteer initiatives. Monica started her career in Washington, DC working in professional and government affairs with the American Association for Clinical Chemistry and worked with Washtenaw County Human Services Collaborative in Ann Arbor, Michigan before joining Pfizer.

Monica is a licensed foster care parent and has served on numerous not-for-profit boards. In 2016, she was recognized as a Young Hispanic Corporate Achiever by the Hispanic Association on Corporate Responsibility. In 2011, Monica was named the United Way of Southeastern Connecticut Campaign Coordinator of the Year after helping to raise over two million dollars for the organization.

She holds a master's degree in public policy and a bachelor's degree in kinesiology, both from the University of Michigan.

Monica Tijerina

Corporate Social Responsibility Strategist

Years in HR: 14

Monica.Tijerina@us.mcd.com

LinkedIn.com/in/tijerinam/

TEN LESSONS

BY FRANCISCA PHILLIPS

"Say 'Yes'! Then figure it out."

From a very young age I was indoctrinated with the belief that I should be learning my entire life. During my childhood, my parents were a strong influence. In young adulthood, I had numerous experiences that reinforced that outlook. As a professional on my career adventure, I continue to not only encounter "a-ha moments" – I am now actively evangelizing this learning mindset to my peers, collaborators, and protégés. These are my ten lessons.

LIFE LESSONS

I went to an English-speaking school. During my high school year, the British Embassy offered an opportunity to participate in a survival weekend. I missed the word "survival" and only focused on the other information: long walks in nature, exploration, campfire stories, and team-building activities. I had never been on a campout, so my mom encouraged me to take advantage of this opportunity.

We were dropped off in a remote area. We were given a live chicken to care for. (We named her Tipi). Then the forced marches started. We had to cross a stream by swinging from a rope. Those who did not have the upper-body strength got quite wet. We had to figure out how to build a fire inside a circle of stones – without matches. We had to make a place to sleep - without tents. And then we had to make our dinner – Tipi.

I did not eat that weekend. I did not sleep much lying on the cold, hard ground. I was not very happy-go-lucky during the physical team challenges. Hangry, sleep-deprived Francisca is not a fun person. My throat hurt from dehydration, my muscles hurt from the physical exertion, and no one cared. When we emerged from the wilderness on Sunday afternoon, I saw my parents approaching. That is when I started crying (without tears because of the dehydration). In a hoarse voice, I tried to tell them about everything that happened – and how horrible it was. My mom patiently listened and then said something that I anchor to every time I face a significantly frustrating challenge, *"If you survived this weekend then you can survive anything."* And thus far, she has been absolutely right.

I wanted to earn money during college, so the university helped me get a job tutoring English. What was meant to be relatively easy work because I had a special skill turned into a passion. I loved working with children. I loved seeing them gain confidence as they improved. And I gained a boost to my self-esteem as everyone kept recommending me to others. It was obvious that I needed to learn more about teaching – which led to my master's degree. *Curiosity often leads to an undiscovered passion.*

During a trip to the U.S., I met my now husband of twenty years. We had two dates before I had to go back home to Chile. We had an eighteen-month, long-distance relationship before we got married. I was very worried that I was going to leave my Chilean life behind. However, at home we speak both languages – Spanish when I am mad, of course. Thanksgiving is followed by *Noche Buena*, Christmas, and Chilean New Year's traditions. *You're not leaving your life behind; you bring your life with you.*

CAREER LESSONS

I wanted to get a job on my own and leverage my extensive education once I got to the U.S. One of the consulting firms that my husband worked with was looking for some help. The owner asked me if I could create a PowerPoint deck. I said, "Yes." Fortunately, this was late on a Friday so I had the weekend to learn how to use PowerPoint. He was impressed with the deck and hired me. The next challenge was to translate human resources consulting documents into Spanish. I had to quickly find all of the vocabulary in Spanish, which was challenging because I was not familiar with this lingo. He was impressed so he asked me to learn how to be the administrator for multi-rater assessment (a.k.a. 360) software. I took classes and figured it out. That led to me training other people how to use that same software and delivering presentations to potential clients and at conferences – in English and Spanish. One of the biggest transitions for me personally and professionally was that I found that by the end of working for this consulting firm I was no longer submissive and deferential when speaking Spanish. I was speaking Spanish like I was speaking English – with confidence and bravado. That would have never happened if I had responded with, "I have never used PowerPoint." Say, *"Yes!" then figure it out.*

My first corporate position after becoming a mom was as an HR specialist. With an on-site daycare this was the perfect situation. However, a lot of professionals – especially other women – criticized me for staying in the role of specialist for nine years. But I had a boss that understood me and my life. She was a terrific motivator and practiced what our department preached about recognizing great work and great results. She gave me the flexibility that I needed to attend school events for my sons and my vacations could align with what worked best for my families in the U.S. and Chile. I had numerous opportunities to move into other areas of the company, and other companies, where I might make more money or have a larger title, but what was most important to me at that point in my life was my family and having a great place to work. I have no regrets about those nine years; they were a blessing. *Do what you enjoy – especially if you get the flexibility you need.*

Once my boys got older, I was ready for a promotion. I proved that my work had evolved into more project management and data analysis. I was primarily focused on employee engagement and the executives wanted the company to win a spot on a "great place to work" list. I pitched the HR leaders on the need for a dedicated role to take ownership of the employee engagement survey, which would also tie nicely into the work required to put the company on the list. They knew my work ethic from the prior nine years and agreed with my proposal. *Create your own future role by proving it will add value.*

A new chief human resources officer (CHRO) arrived after I had only spent a year as an analyst. He quickly realized that I could help him navigate the org chart and learn how the company operated. I was his go-to person for some key initiatives. For example, he wanted to launch five new benefits for all employees every year – even though I did not have any knowledge or experience with benefits. Like my first full-time job when I landed in the U.S., I said, "Yes." However, this time I had a champion that knew what I did not know, and he gave me assignments to stretch my skills. He helped me become comfortable with being uncomfortable. I went through two years of intensive professional growth and I also earned my first nickname – Shiny Shoes. *Get a sponsor or mentor that will challenge you.*

I partnered with someone from sales to create a Diversity and Inclusion (D&I) Team. Neither of us had any knowledge or experience with D&I so we started networking with leaders from companies that had a positive reputation in that field. We figured out what would work in our corporate culture and launched several programs. My boss started touting our industry involvement and new initiatives openly. He taught me to put myself out there and highlight my accomplishments. He would always say, *"It's not bragging when it's the truth, and no one notices the silent ones."*

INTERPERSONAL LESSONS

As a Hispanic woman, I have experienced misunderstandings that could have resulted in frustration or feelings of being the victim of bias. However, from my very early days of travel and the many conversations and stories that I have heard, I know that people don't always understand and are not intentionally trying to hurt someone. Most of the time they are simply curious or confused. People have said that they thought Chile was a spicy dish made of ground beef and beans. In Texas, because I spoke Spanish, people assumed I was from Mexico. When I was getting my driver's license and I checked-off "white" as my race, I was told I was not white - I had to select Hispanic. People have asked, "What do your people wear/eat/celebrate?" When people say I am not American, I like to tell them, "I am. I am South American." And, more recently, someone asked me how I could be both white and Hispanic, which led me to teach them about the difference between race and ethnicity. I know that these people are all trying to understand, so I take these opportunities to teach them about myself and my background. This is easy to do when I *assume positive intent.*

When COVID-19 resulted in a three-month furlough, I was very upset. However, it gave me an opportunity to help my husband with his children's books. I learned a lot of new skills that were immediately applicable when I was called back to work. I learned how books are designed, I was able to practice being an editor, I built a website from scratch, and I dabbled in graphic design. Life is not perfect, but we can make it work if we want to. *Make it work for you.*

REFLECT AND RISE

My story contains ten different lessons. Pause and answer these questions to reflect on your own life lessons.

1. What are the top five lessons from your life and career?

2. What "survival story" do you have that helps you keep going when things get rough?

3. What should you be asking for that you haven't? Think of a request that is reasonable and important to you, but you have convinced yourself is a waste of time to pursue. Write it down. Now, pick a date, time, and place when you will make the ask:

Date: _____ Time: _____ Place: _____

BIOGRAPHY

Francisca is a native of Santiago, Chile. She has been a teacher, flight attendant, interpreter for international delegations and ambassadors, leadership development consultant, and is currently an HR professional. Her human resources career encompasses external leadership assessment and development consulting as well as 15 years in corporate HR. She started off focused on rewards and recognition, took ownership of the employee engagement survey, and helped to reestablish a D&I function.

Francisca helped create the Diversity Leadership Network (DLN) and is a frequent speaker and panel member at HR and D&I conferences and events. She earned a B.S. in Translation and Interpretation, a master's degree in education, a certificate in environmental studies, and a diploma from the Diplomatic Academy. She and her husband are writing books that teach children how to thrive in life. Her most important accomplishments are being a mother of two boys, Garret and Santiago, and an abuela to her grandbaby, Elliot. Francisca lives in Key Biscayne with her husband and their dog named Rabbit.

Francisca Phillips

Engagement, Diversity & Inclusion Leader

Years in HR: 15

francisca.phillips@gmail.com

Instagram: @shinyshoesstyle

BY IRMA I. REYES

"Leaders learn from experience and challenge themselves to raise the bar."

This is my reflection, my story on how I was strategically placed with people, spaces, and places that led to my current role as director of human resources for a domestic violence organization which oversees a large network of eighteen other domestic violence entities in Connecticut. I can't help but remember that almost nineteen years ago, when I was twenty-eight years old, I wrote in my personal journal about the many struggles of women in leadership. As I read my own words on how much I admired female journalists and reporters in the public eye, it was truly an emotional moment for me.

I know now that I once relied on television to show me what successful women in leadership looked like. In my journal I wrote:

"I know women are given leadership opportunities, but I also know they are difficult to get. These women have become successful, regardless of the obstacles, time, and effort I know are required to get to where they are. Were they just lucky?"

I interpret my quote to mean that the women who inspired me with their success did so regardless of their adversities. I presumed the women I saw on television were like the many young women like me, and experienced the same challenges and obstacles growing up, yet somehow found a way to their dream career and passion. I asked myself, if it took luck to succeed, would I ever be that lucky?

THE POWER OF OPPORTUNITY

My leadership journey started back in high school, when out of all of the seniors in my class, the assistant principal selected me to participate in an internship program at Yale University. I was surprised, since I wasn't an honor student, but I was the only person selected that year, nonetheless. While this may seem normal to many, my parents and I were incredibly grateful for the opportunity.

Had the assistant principal not approached me, I may never have experienced an internship. At the time, I did not have access to a computer at home, and we did not have internet. My parents, who were bilingual, mostly spoke Spanish. They worked day and evening jobs, and while they were my very first mentors who always told me "education is something no one could ever take away from you, learn as much as you can," they relied on me to push forward and seek out additional opportunities.

What was the big deal about the internship opportunity? Simply put, it placed me in an unexpected role that opened doors to employment at the university. I worked as an assistant computer analyst intern, which led to my hiring as a permanent file clerk there after graduation. This overwhelming, positive experience was motivational and empowering to me.

For some people who see themselves represented within a respected institution, this feeling may not be relatable. However, when you live in a community filled with gun violence, drugs, and a variety of crimes that are commonplace and you are faced with this reality every time you walk out the door, it is challenging to reframe your "normal" and actually believe you go to work every day at a safe, prestigious, respected institution.

THE VALUE OF MENTORS

The purpose of my leadership and my desire to lead as a servant leader, were values given to me through the example of my life mentors. I met my career mentor while working at Yale. She was transparent and genuine. Within the first few months of working with her, she said, "Irma, I grew up in the same neighborhood you live in and I know what it is like." To me, those words were a huge sigh of relief and it was the start of my trust in her. She gave me opportunities, even though I still spoke with a noticeable accent. She treated me with respect for my upbringing and culture.

"You're given opportunities because of your work ethic and that is why we are a team," she said.

She made it clear no one gives anything to you. You have to put in the work first. Without a doubt, when it came to developing my leadership abilities, she was a huge influence on me.

If you read my bio, you will see it says that I am a determined driver of diversity and inclusion in the workforce. Being self-motivated, this statement speaks to my life experiences and how important it was, and still is, to feel included. In what way was inclusion important to my life, you ask?

There I was in my twenties, with a great job in a management role. I thought I was going in the direction I wanted, and everything was wonderful! But then, my mentor retired. It was at that time I found myself on my own, trying to find my way in my career, *solita* (alone).

Finding my way was a rebirth, without my mentor, who

by the way was a Caucasian woman of Italian heritage. I began noticing who I was, and immediately it hit me like a storm. I was the only Latina in my work environment. I had not noticed it before because my mentor was someone I could relate to and who was supportive and a trusted advisor. Her absence opened my eyes to the reality that I "made" it into a workforce that did not look like me. My bright days became very sad.

Perhaps I should have been proud to be the only Latina in the board room. What do you think? The boardroom had a long, redwood table and large, comfortable, black, leather seats. For a moment, as I sat there with an agenda in my hand, I thought, *wow, I am the girl I see on television! Could this be me growing into positions that allow me to have an impact in the workplace and in life?*

But what good was it to sit in the seat where I felt I could not voice my thoughts and ideas? There were days I cried on my way to work and finally, when speaking to HR, they acknowledged my sentiment. I was told they were working on restructuring the institution to be more inclusive. I felt a sense of belonging when my concerns about lack of diversity were validated. I am grateful for the experiences and opportunities I had earned in my position, but feeling like the only Latina in the work environment was very uncomfortable. This was my turning point, and I chose to do something about it.

A LEAP OF FAITH

I took a leap of faith, even though I was scared. I have always believed that sometimes events happen to get you where you need to be. I chose to give my notice and find a place elsewhere, not knowing where I would land. I knew one thing—I was not a quitter and in my next career, I would make positive change. I read motivational podcasts, books, and speeches, and increased my inspiration and confidence! It was then I launched my career in civil rights programs and diversity and inclusion (D&I).

I knew I would have to start over if I wanted to change my career and begin to gain experience serving employees and agencies with equal employment opportunities and D&I. I began my breakthrough with fear, focus, drive, and determination. Within six months of volunteering with the Connecticut Office of the Secretary of the State, I was hired full-time. This is where I began my new career, which allowed me to advocate for employees in the field of equal employment opportunity and diversity. I have enforced civil rights laws, implemented Affirmative Action programs, and conducted investigations of disparate treatment and sexual harassment. I routinely provided D&I and sexual harassment training to hundreds of employees. Amazingly, I have always had a great fear of public speaking, and now it has become part of my everyday role.

As the human resource director for the Connecticut

Coalition of Domestic Violence, I am directly responsible for the overall administration and coordination of the human resources functions associated with growing and transforming the organization. In this role, I live my passion to eradicate racial and ethnic disparities. I also conduct workforce analysis and am responsible for cultural recruitment and leadership development programs for an inclusive workforce.

People like to feel valued and they like feedback; they want to know they are making an impact or they are an integral part of the agency, regardless of their race, color, or national origin.

One the biggest lessons I learned early on in my career is to listen. In order to gain trust in any institution, I must first be well informed enough about the people and the work so that when I am making decisions, I am able to essentially help the institution and the employees be sensitive to cultural diversity. In the book *Leading Without Power*, which I read in my master's program, the author says, "trust begins with a personal commitment to respect others, to take everyone seriously. Respect demands that we first recognize each other's gifts, strengths, and interests, and then we integrate them into the work of the organization."

My past experiences shaped me into the leader that I am today. R. Quinn in *Moments of Greatness: Entering* the *Fundamental State of Leadership* says, "Leaders do their best work when they have reached their fundamental state of leadership." This means, for example, when you made mistakes and were punished for them as a child, you learned from your experiences and now want to make a positive difference in life. These lessons can influence your actions when you face a significant life challenge, a promotional opportunity, the risk of professional failure, divorce, or death of a loved one. Leaders learn from experience and challenge themselves to raise the bar.

This was my fundamental state when I found myself being the only Latina and being seen and not heard. It was then that this fundamental state determined my life's path and I left my institution after ten years of hard work and effort.

This is where I am now, finding who I am as a leader, in a place where I am taking everything that I have learned that works, including all of the lessons learned from previous challenges, work ethics, and emotional behavior and humbleness, and applying it to my life today.

My children, now young adults motivate me. My daughter, who has a full-time career in healthcare, and also runs her own online fashion business. My son has aspirations to run a commercial real estate empire in New York City and cultivate podcasts for sharing his experiences on what it is like to have financial freedom. Also, I would be remiss if I didn't mention my career in human resources. Serving employees so they feel empowered, validated, and recognized in the workplace is one of my biggest motivators.

REFLECT AND RISE

I would like to offer some advice to those Latinas seeking careers in HR.

1. **Lead with confidence!** This means believing in yourself so much that you are not stirred by the thoughts of others; rather, you continuously remind yourself you are worthy of all great things.

2. **Find yourself a mentor.** No matter how old or young you are, we all need a line of support.

3. **Address your questions.** Have you experienced points in your life where you have asked yourself, "Who am I? What is my purpose? What do I stand for?" If these are your questions, start your journey to discovery by writing detailed answers to those questions in your journal to help guide you to your answers of self- discovery.

4. **Stand tall, chin up, smile, and always love yourself.** Practice self-confidence and see how it will empower you over time. When you talk about your goals, wishes, and desires, I hope you know you will not get there only with luck. You have to lead confidently, take a leap of faith, and work for it.

BIOGRAPHY

Irma I. Reyes is a determined driver of diversity and inclusion who began her career at the Connecticut Office of the Secretary of the State, Division of Human Resources where she ensured equal access to recruitment programs and business owners securing opportunities with the state. At the Connecticut Department of Transportation, she received a leadership award and managed the Title VI and Limited English Proficiency programs.

Irma also served the Connecticut Department of Children and Families (DCF), Office of Diversity and Equity, where she helped implement the agency's Affirmative Action Programs and their compliance with Title VII and other civil rights laws. During her tenure there, Irma received an award for Multicultural Competency and Racial Justice.

Irma is now the human resource director for the Connecticut Coalition Against Domestic Violence and is responsible for the overall human resources functions associated with growing and transforming the organization. She is the chairperson for their Diversity Action Team and leads ongoing initiatives to educate and recognize diversity. Her role involves conducting workforce analysis, cultural recruitment, and implementing leadership development programs for inclusivity in the workforce.

Irma holds a B.S in Business Management and a M.S. in Management and Organizational Leadership.

Irma I. Reyes

Director of HR

Years in HR: 13

irmareyes.business@gmail.com

Instagram: @hello.irma

RIDING THE WAVES OF CHANGE

BY KARINA A. JIMENEZ

"We need self-care to succeed professionally and personally."

I have always been an overachiever. In grammar school, I wouldn't accept anything less than A's. I even got my gym teacher to change my B to an A on my report card. Then I was admitted to a selective high school where I was no longer in the top one percent of my class. It was the beginning of a challenging journey.

LEARNING EXPERIENCE

My parents, some of the most intelligent, hardworking individuals I know, never attended college, but always encouraged us to go to college away from home. I was the first in my immediate family to leave, and I'll always remember my parents packing up my aunt's van to move me into my dorm at the University of Illinois in Urbana-Champaign. I had craved freedom for so long, yet I was terrified.

My first year in college was difficult. I struggled academically, and also with time management, discipline, etc. I quickly learned that the institution was not built to support me. I needed to find what I would call my "hustle," which manifested itself in many ways. I obtained a job to earn money for entertainment and books, and I took a position with the America Reads, America Counts program, located off-campus. I would work into the wee morning hours, then woke just hours later to catch a bus to my assignment.

I also enrolled in tutoring, and I was always on the go, and hardly ever rested or took time to tend my physical, mental, emotional, or spiritual needs. Then in March 2008, my cousin had a severe car accident that left him in a vegetative state before he died. One of my uncles became a victim of gun violence, and another uncle experienced a debilitating stroke. I remember understanding these incidents for what they were—a story told over the phone. I took the Greyhound bus home, for my cousin's funeral, and returned to another world on campus. I never truly allowed myself the time to grieve or process each incident. Instead, I just bottled them up unaware that I would be forced to process these unexpectedly.

I was taking my last final exam of the semester when I began to sweat profusely and shake in my seat. My mouth become incredibly dry, and I had a butterfly feeling in my chest. I didn't understand what I was feeling. I begged and pleaded to use the restroom and got some water but returned to the room still feeling uneasy. Back at my seat, I could no longer stay in that room. To this day, I remember how quickly I raced through those questions just to get out. I needed air. I needed to escape. I submitted my test, ran out of the room, and dashed to the bus stop.

As I waited, the rain only amplified my anxiety. I couldn't wait there any longer; I didn't feel well, I was losing control, and that feeling was too foreign to me. I'm grateful my friend came to my rescue and drove me back to the dorm, my heart pounding incessantly. I was convinced that I was dying, so I pleaded with her to take me to the hospital. The physicians confirmed that I was not dying; I had experienced my first panic attack. I was released from the hospital an hour later, and two days later I returned to Chicago. I had completed my first year of college, panic attack and all.

RISE AND FALL

That day changed my life. The paralyzing fear of having another panic attack plagues my body and mind to this day. After returning home, I was diagnosed with Generalized Anxiety Disorder (G.A.D.). G.A.D. can be hard to manage on its own, but coupled with my overachieving, Type-A personality, it can be a recipe for disaster. That summer, I worked on my mental health and self-care, and learned that there were many factors that contributed to my first attack. I had been exhausted and dealing with unprocessed trauma from my family tragedies. I worked to identify my triggers, how to cope with stress, and manage my disorder so I could return to school in the fall and be successful.

The next three years were full of professional and personal developmental opportunities. I was constantly working on becoming a better version of myself. I found my niche at *La Casa Cultural Latina (La Casa)*, a safe space on campus for Latinx students. They really understood my struggles as a Latina woman in a predominantly white institution. La Casa became mi casa on campus, where I interacted with those I called my sisters and brothers at the university. This was the support system I so desperately needed.

La Casa would uplift me on the days I had nothing left to give and give to me when I felt I could no longer receive. Most importantly, the community molded me into a strong Latina leader. I learned how to be my own advocate and became more involved with the Latinx community, on and off campus. I learned the power of community and inspiration. La Casa ended up opening doors that shaped me professionally, as a network of people who supported, pushed, and linked me to opportunities. I was shown ways to develop my civic engagement skills, governmental knowledge, and personal growth. I interned with the United States Hispanic Leadership Institute (USHLI) where I was named Outstanding Intern. I was selected as one of sixteen interns nationwide for the Congressional Internship Program at the Congressional Hispanic Caucus Institute (CHCI). These experiences opened my eyes to the work that needed to be done within the Latinx community.

After college, I obtained my first full-time position as a case manager for *Carreras en Salud* (Careers in Healthcare), a nationally recognized career pathway program, at *Instituto del Progreso Latino* (Instituto), a nonprofit located in the southwest side of Chicago, between two prominent Latino communities, Pilsen and Little Village. It put me on the forefront of doing community work with the neediest individuals. That year I also obtained a part-time position as a special projects assistant for the Cook County Commissioner of the 7th District, and enrolled in graduate school at Northwestern University. I was on fire to make a difference, but the fire dimmed when I suffered a second debilitating panic attack. This attack grounded me and taught me about a new trigger—major life changes.

CHALLENGE AND REWARD

I recovered, and after one year of serving as a case manager, Instituto asked me to serve as the organization grants compliance specialist—as one of two first hires in a brand-new department. I assisted program directors in managing their programmatic budgets, which included revenue streams from public and private donors. I managed programmatic and grant deliverables and outcomes and helped administer the organizations system database. A year later I was tapped on the shoulder by the director of human resources to join her team as an HR generalist, which started my HR career.

Two months into the role, the director told me she would be resigning, which was devastating because I had joined the team to learn from her. Soon afterwards, the CEO pulled me into his office.

"Karina, you're going to be the face of this department," he said.

"There's no way," I replied, incredulously. "I am just not experienced for this role."

He said that I would be fine and had what it took to succeed in this position. He reassured me I had the support of my *Instituto Familia*, and my family and friends. I needed to believe in myself as my community believed in me.

The beginning was challenging yet rewarding. I worked with a woman who had a language barrier with her supervisor and needed a medical leave but was incredibly afraid to lose her position. As I told her that she had rights as an employee, I could sense her relief at having someone on her side. She took her medical leave and upon her return, she brought me *nopales* to express her gratitude. This generous act overwhelmed me, knowing she was barely making enough to make ends meet, yet she gave me a gift. I understood the value of my work, and I realized that my experience with the Latino community had given me special insight into their specific concerns and needs. With the good, came the challenging. At the beginning, a leader told me I was not addressing employee relation concerns fast enough because I preferred to observe to make strides towards meaningful change. The leader called this "riding the waves." At the moment, I didn't understand what she meant, but now I know she meant riding waves of change as a Latina in a professional environment. I did, and still do ride waves of change.

After a year I had gained the organization's trust and became the human resources manager. I was now the face of the department, leading a small but mighty team that serviced a nonprofit, two charter high schools, and a college. I had to deliver, even without a departmental budget. Through these challenges, I built my toolbox of skills. I was a bilingual, bicultural, resourceful, negotiating machine, and brought meaningful change to our department.

SELF CARE FOR SUCCESS

Culturally, Latinos are taught the value of *respeto* which manifests itself in many ways. For me, in the workplace, this value was reflected in the form of obeying individuals with authority and never saying no, which made it difficult to set boundaries and advocate for myself. There were times I became so consumed with being the best HR manager and gaining a name for myself that my physical and mental wellbeing suffered. Physically, I was unrecognizable. Mentally, my anxiety symptoms and panic attacks were more frequent. Socially, my long-standing friendships slowly diminished. I did not understand that we need self-care to succeed professionally and personally. Now, I understand the importance of making myself a priority and the importance of self-care. By prioritizing my wellbeing, my physical, mental, and emotional needs are tended to, lessening my overall stress, improving my productivity in my personal and professional life, ultimately allowing me to do what I enjoy most, serving my community. I learned that I needed to advocate for myself as much as I advocated for others. I also learned that it was ok to still value my cultural beliefs but to do so in a way that was healthy, breaking down generational mentalities that didn't align with my personal beliefs. I made it a point to carve out my own identity in the workplace as a Latina millennial.

My time at *Instituto* ended after eight meaningful years of serving my community. Currently, I serve as a vicariate (regional) human resources manager for the Archdiocese of Chicago. I'm blessed to be able to use all my skills to serve more than sixty parishes and schools. Even so, there are times that I find myself starting all over again and feeling as if I have to work twice as hard to earn my seat at the table. It's draining, but I remind myself I've overcome it in the past and can again. As I ride the waves of change, the unknown lies ahead, but I know my next step will be calculated and rooted in the values I have gained from working in my community. My community got me here and I believe that as long as I remain true to myself and my guided purpose, I will welcome the next step, recognize it as an opportunity to achieve my greatest potential, and continue to be a driving force as a Latina human resources professional.

REFLECT AND RISE

- **Often ask yourself and evaluate:**
  - Who is part of your community that is contributing to your personal and professional growth?
  - What self-care practices are you engaging in to protect your physical, mental, and spiritual wellbeing?

- **On Karina's Bookshelf:**
  - *Year of Yes* by Shonda Rhimes
  - *The Four Agreements* by Don Miguel Ruiz
  - *Resilience* by the Harvard Business Review

BIOGRAPHY

Karina A. Jimenez currently serves as the vicariate (regional) human resources manager at the Archdiocese of Chicago, serving more than sixty parishes and schools. Prior to joining the archdioceses, Karina worked at *Instituto del Progreso Latino*, a non-profit located on the southwest side of Chicago. She has vast experience in non-profit management and in the government sector. She has experience in case management, grant management, policy development, and human resource management. She obtained her B.A. in Urban and Regional Planning from the University of Illinois at Urbana-Champaign and her master's degree in public policy and administration from Northwestern University. She is also a SHRM- senior certified professional in HR. Karina also serves on Midtown Educational Foundation's Auxiliary Board.

In her spare time, Karina enjoys spending time with her family, bargain hunting, and exploring different neighborhoods in Chicago. She also enjoys hosting themed get togethers, crafting, and an occasional DIY project.

Karina A. Jimenez

Regional HR Manager

Years in HR: 6

karina.a.jimenez@gmail.com

LinkedIn.com/in/Karina-a-Jimenez/

WHEN THE STARS ALIGN

BY SUSANA MOTA

"Although situations you are in can make it very difficult for you, the responsibility for change falls on you."

Growing up, I always knew that I would pursue a career that allowed me the opportunity to help others. However, I was never clear on exactly how I could do that or what it looked like for me. I was often asked about my passions and my ideal career. My response was always that my career had to be one in which I make an impact and have the opportunity to help others. This has been my mission and goal in life. I want to impact others in a positive way, regardless of what challenges I face.

CULTURE SHOCK

After graduating high school, I was ready for all the challenges, or so I thought. I began my college career at Indiana University-Bloomington (IUB) as a young, eighteen-year-old Latina from East Chicago, Indiana. Growing up, I was surrounded by individuals who looked like me or had experiences similar to mine. It wasn't until my freshman year of college, where I faced a culture shock. I was in a campus with more than thirty-seven thousand students with probably about twenty percent of them being domestic students of color. It didn't seem like a big issue, until it was. How could someone like me make sure I succeeded in such an environment? I was fortunate to have my older siblings on campus who were able to introduce me to important resources along the way. I had to find my own circle, my own support, to make sure I succeeded.

Like many Latinas, I was also very close to my family and friends growing up. I had to find my new circle of support but also maintain those relationships that were important to me. On top of all that, I had to find ways to pay for college and maintain my well-being. It was all very stressful, but failure was just not an option.

I sought out people similar to me, whether they shared my cultural background, my academic program, or enjoyed the same hobbies as me. Eventually, I connected to many student organizations and found the support I needed at the Latino Cultural center, where I met many close friends who later became my family. I overcame one of many obstacles keeping me from success in school.

Four years later, I graduated from IUB with a degree in human development and family studies. To many, that would be successful in itself, but my mission wasn't completed. I began looking into nonprofits and social services to fulfill my values and beliefs and serve an organization that aligned with my academic achievement. This landed me my first "real world job" as a service coordinator for an early intervention program serving children and their families in the community. I was able to give back to the families from my hometown, serving children from zero to three years of age who had developmental delays. Since the families were struggling, I decided to help assist families further during the holidays by fundraising.

During one of my efforts, my car was broken into and the donations I had been collecting were stolen. Devastated, I couldn't let this fail. As an organization, we were able to fundraise for dozens of families, which filled me with joy. Throughout the year, I always felt there was more I could and should be doing to further help serve the community. Therefore, I felt the need to further my education.

ASKING FOR HELP

With that mindset, I made my way to Northern Arizona University (NAU) to earn a master's degree in early childhood education. I equated having more education with opening more doors to help me serve the community on a larger scale. As I made my way to Arizona from Indiana, I found myself again away from the majority of my family and friends. I focused on my education and career, but something greater surfaced. For years, I had covered my depression and anxiety with a smile on my face and the need to take care of others. While yes, I still wanted to take care of others, I wouldn't be able to do so if I didn't take care of myself first.

I hid my depression because it is something that is not openly talked about in the Latino community. I was now living many states away from my family, encountering personal battles, insecurities, anger issues, and healing from a past miscarriage. It all hit me like a ton of bricks. The time was now and if I wanted to continue to help others, I had to help none other than myself.

Coincidentally, I was working in behavioral health as I attended NAU. I became a family support specialist that offered therapeutic help for individuals who faced issues similar to mine. It was meant to be; I was able to confide in peers that specialized in my problems and this led me to look into finding my own therapist.

Asking for help doesn't make you a weaker person; it makes you human. For the longest time, I did not want to ask for help, but looking back, I wish I had done so sooner.

After getting the help I needed, I successfully graduated from NAU, but I knew I had to make my way back to Indiana.

This is when I was introduced to a hotel management company by a friend who told me about an opening in their human resources department for a corporate associate relations manager. With uncertainty, I applied and was hired.

To say that I have always pursued human resources would be a lie. However, unbeknownst to me, HR is the career path I was meant to take. It is where I am able to assist individuals of all walks of life on a daily basis and make a true impact. In this role I have met individuals from many walks of life, including those who are relieved to hear a Spanish-speaking voice on the other end of the phone when they are facing challenges at their job. I had a group of housekeepers once call to thank me and say how proud they were of me to have *"un trabajo asi"* (such a job!) in the corporate office. They felt the comfort in someone who cared and wanted to work with them to face their challenges. Whether they were facing a termination, a write-up, a suspension, medical leave, or pay issues, they knew they had someone they could confide in who would make sure they understood the process.

THE "HUMAN" IN HR

I believe we need more "human" in human resources. When we do not see those who "look like us," it can be discouraging, but sharing stories about experiences may open doors to many. If you do not see someone who looks like you in a higher-level position, why can't it be you? Why not climb that ladder and help others join you along the way?

My work in both nonprofit early intervention and behavioral health prepared me for my work in HR and shaped me to handle some of the intense situations in HR that I have faced. At the end of the day, we are all human and everyone is going through something in their life that can impact them. My prior jobs have made me more empathetic to individuals I encounter daily.

In my current position, I have been faced with yet another obstacle that could easily tear me down. As of May 2020, I was let go from my job after months of being furloughed. When I joined this corporation, I had hoped to be with the company for a very long time and continue to grow and develop. Unfortunately, COVID-19 had claimed the jobs of many, and now it claimed mine as well. It was very stressful as I was moving to a new home with my daughter and her father, and bills continued to pour in.

While this is a stressful time, I also consider it a gift. I am taking this time for not only my daughter, but her future as well. I am studying to finally take the SHRM certification test that I have put off for more than two years. I am planning my next steps in my career and recently completed a certification program in hospitality and tourism management. In addition to that, I completed a fourteen-week women's leadership program which I also put off for years. I continued to make excuses for myself but came to the realization that the time has, and always will be, now. Tomorrow is not always guaranteed so make the time to better yourself.

Though my educational path has been indirect, I found my pathway to human resources through the relationships I developed. Throughout my journey I have experienced trials and tribulations that may have steered me away from success. However, I chose to ignore the obstacles and instead empower myself to continue improving and impacting those around me. I could have easily dropped out of college at IUB and settled for the jobs I had. However, although situations you are in in can make it very difficult for you, the responsibility for change falls on you. For me, I chose to create my support system from where I was and used it to keep me grounded. I faced mental health issues and after years of hiding them, I chose to face them. Nobody is going to fight for you other than YOU! I will not let any obstacles slow me down.

Everything falls into place at the right time, whether

you believe it or not. In my journey, I felt that I had lost my support system, lost myself mentally, and even reached the point of losing my job. These moments could easily break anybody, but I resisted that urge and allowed these moments to mold and strengthen me to become the individual I am today. There will continue to be tests in life, and moments of clouded thoughts are inevitable. As they occur, keep your head up and never forget your overall goal and mission in life. It is your responsibility to change it and not settle. Don't be afraid of the unknown and get comfortable with the uncomfortable before moving forward. Take that risk, challenge yourself, and move to the best you can be!

REFLECT AND RISE

If you find yourself in a situation that you are unhappy with, ask:

1. Does the situation align with your own personal values and beliefs?
2. Do you have an internal battle you need to face first?
3. What steps do you need to take to better your future?

As you answer these questions, you will watch the stars align for you.

BIOGRAPHY

Born and raised in East Chicago, Indiana, Susana Mota is the youngest of five siblings and had the opportunity to watch them all work hard for their success. Susana had the support of two loving parents who showed her that no matter what situation she encountered; hard work would always be worth it at the end. She is setting a similar example for her almost two-year-old daughter.

In high school, she was the student that enjoyed keeping busy with her job as a waitress, student organizations and sports, yet always found time to spend with friends and family. That same mindset continued into her college years, as she would always keep a jam-packed schedule working multiple jobs and serving on the board of many student organizations.

After building a successful career as a HR professional, Susana recently found herself laid off from her job as the corporate HR business partner for a hotel management company due to impact of the COVID-19 global pandemic. While she currently finds herself joining those who are unemployed, this has not, and will not stop her from her success.

Susana Mota

HR Business Partner

Years in HR: 4

motasusana524@gmail.com

219-902-2164

CREATE YOUR OWN PATH

BY LUZ PEREZ

"Don't wait for someone else to open the door for you; seek and create your own path."

I immigrated to the United States at age thirteen and was off to college at seventeen. Though naïve and living in a new country, I developed big dreams. I always pictured myself suited up in a big corner office. As I got older and lived in the reality of being a poor, Spanish-speaking Latina with limited resources, those dreams slowly drifted away. I eventually found my way, but my journey wasn't quite as smooth as I expected.

During my first three years in the U.S., I learned about the importance and scrutiny of working hard to achieve what you want. Growing up in a single-parent Latino household, with a strict mother who worked two jobs, my siblings and I had to pull our own weight around the house. As I had an extreme sense of independence, making the decision to go to college two hundred miles away from home was easy.

As an undergrad at Binghamton University, I spent the first two years celebrating a new-found freedom. I focused on taking elective courses and tried out classes in psychology and sociology. I hated spending days in lecture classes of four hundred students, learning about things that I'd probably never use. During school breaks I didn't want to go home, so I worked as a student counselor and held a part-time job at JCPenney to support myself.

At the start of my junior year, I received a letter that stated, "Action required-- you must declare a major, or you will lose your financial aid." I couldn't afford college without the loans. How was I supposed to elect a major not knowing who I was or what I wanted? Who knows what they want at nineteen?

THE POWER OF ASKING

I glanced through my course catalog and picked sociology. I couldn't let these years go to waste, and I wanted to make my mom proud. Having a diploma would beat the Latino statistics and help me get a job.

While completing course requirements, I joined a sorority, Hermandad de Sigma Iota Alpha, Inc. to ground myself with principles of leadership and community work, because at least it gave me purpose. I maintained my summer jobs and took active roles in several organizations. On December 2004, I did it! I earned my degree, but then I had to ask myself, now what?

I made the decision to stay in school to figure out my next move. I wasn't ready to go back home with a degree and no plan, but I enjoyed being a student counselor, so I enrolled in a master's degree program at the university that focused on student affairs and diversity. I hoped this could at least be the first step in discovering who I was meant to be.

The program required three internships, and I didn't know how I could obtain one. The guidance I received was to just go and ask! You can always learn what you do not know.

In February of 2005, I walked into the Office of Graduate Admissions and met with an administrator. I asked if I could work there in exchange for internship credit. I was immediately offered the opportunity to revise outdated policies. I hesitated, because as a previous ESL student, how could I write policies? But now that I asked, I couldn't say no. I bought a dictionary and began my very first HR- related experience. I updated the Graduate Admissions Student Policy Handbook, and I felt so proud – look at me, a poor, Spanish-speaking Latina revising university policies! Nobody reads handbooks anyway, but it was an accomplishment and something I had enjoyed.

I obtained a second internship by asking the Health and Safety Department if they needed help, and guess what? They did! I assisted with the documentation of OSHA requirements. I didn't make the connection until after graduation that these were HR experiences.

I completed my master's degree within a year. I packed my bags and made it back home to begin my career and live on my own. I didn't know what type of job I wanted, but when I was introduced to the owners of a healthcare agency, they needed someone to process billing and I asked for the job. I requested information about benefits and the employee handbook, and the HR Director said they did not have one. In fact, they didn't have any onboarding policies in place.

As they grew to fifty employees, the owners hired a consultant to help them implement new policies and I decided to use this as an opportunity. I knew nothing about HR, but I had the aptitude to make things happen. But I always tell people, don't wait for someone else to open the door for you; seek and create your own path. So, I wrote a two-page summary on why I should be selected and handed my proposal to the HR Director; she accepted it with slight modifications because after all, I had zero experience in HR. Like I've said, ask and you shall receive.

I started my new HR Job. I wrote the employee handbook, implemented benefits, created a time recording system and a new orientation program, administered payroll and more. I revamped the HR department with the help of determination and Google. Overall, it was an amazing experience.

We never expect the roadblocks we encounter, but you must know that these obstacles, while difficult, make you much stronger. Reminiscing on my journey, I came across people who wanted to make it difficult for me to succeed; I have vivid memories of bullying and while these experiences caused tears, they helped me rise above, and motivated me to continue to fight, and make intimate self-discoveries.

In 2010, I started to recognize significant contributions I had made in the agency. A new executive was hired to help evolve the business and I saw it as another opportunity to achieve greater results for me and the HR department. I wrote another two-page summary on why I should be promoted to HR Manager based on my contributions, along with information on how I would help evolve our culture and environment. After a couple of months of evaluation, I was promoted. I worked closely with the new executive and together we were able to build a strong foundation for HR and the business partnership. This key relationship helped me secure a seat at the table and taught me so much about the importance of trust. I was finally allowed to add value and I had a strong desire to do more.

CORPORATE AMERICA

At the beginning of 2012, I resigned and planned to move from New York City to Virginia. I took comfort in knowing that this time, I had work-related experience behind me and a pretty good idea of what I wanted to do – it was really the start of my career. I applied to multiple jobs and travelled back and forth for an exhausting six months to attend interviews. Six months later, I received a call to work at a Fortune 200 company. I couldn't believe I had made it to "corporate America."

I wondered if I would be successful, or if I could Google my way through this one? I worried about being able to maintain a good level of authenticity because corporate America was going to be different. Only time would tell. I joined the company as an HR generalist, and it was one of the best decisions I've ever made. Others may have judged me for taking a position which some may construe as a "demotion." I never thought of it that way. It is always more important to look at what you will gain from the experience, than the title you are awarded.

While I joined this new company, I had a manager who motivated me and reminded me that anything was possible when you have the will to learn. My time with her was short because after eight months, she decided to leave. This was a time of reflection for me as I wondered if I could rise to the occasion. A new manager was hired, and

I was determined to make sure my contributions mattered. I took ownership of my development and vocalized what I wanted while executing at high levels. I emerged as a peer leader and a high performer; it felt great to be recognized and empowered. I was engaged and committed, even if that meant sacrificing time with family. My HR hat was on ten hours a day, five days a week, I was promoted to senior generalist, and was on top of my game. Little did I know, I had a way to go.

EVOLVING THROUGH CHANGE

In 2016, I went through another transition. Our mission was to evolve our strategic support across the organization. While I overperformed, I wondered what was holding me back from mentoring and managing HR professionals. My new manager then shared the critical feedback that I needed to allow people to get to know me, to enable stronger partnerships. However, coworkers would walk out of the cafeteria if anyone like me from HR walked in, so how could I be myself with people who didn't want to be around me?

I tried to evolve myself by releasing some of the pressures of being a Latina wanting to fit in when we are really meant to stand out. I went from sporting straight hair to curly hair. While interacting with others, I made my conversations less formal. I made jokes and practiced what I preached, like the notion of "just be yourself." I even "allowed" cursing while talking and attended happy hours. As HR professionals, we can appear too rigid because we feel we must serve as examples. As a Latina HR professional, I tried too hard to change in order to be taken seriously. What I have learned since freeing myself is that the inflexibility we provide in being always "on," can be a roadblock to our own success. My approach has completely changed, and it started with allowing others to get to know me.

Between 2017 and 2020, I made several key contributions, but nothing came close to what I did during the pandemic. I started a new rotation in February, and by mid-March, the company announced we were going to work remotely. My kids' school closed and all I could think about was how I'd start new relationships, via video, with two toddlers running around in the background. It was a nightmare waiting to happen. I apologized profusely over their laughs and interruptions because while I am comfortable being me, I needed to retain professionalism and composure while supporting essential employees who needed my attention; we were all learning how to navigate COVID together.

I had to reground myself with principles my mentors shared. I learned to tune out my kids and I found that leaders were understanding, and had their own little nightmares running around. Sometimes it's easier to make assumptions rather than ask questions and establish expectations. Now, as I run meetings, my kids may be in the background pillow fighting, smiling, yelling, and everyone has come to accept that. This has emphasized that it is okay to be transparent and vulnerable, because only then will others learn to trust and support you. In the last six months, while I faced new challenges, I was able to outperform many of my previous accomplishments because this time I am embracing who I am, and comfortable with what I know I can bring to the table.

My transformation over the years has been inspired by amazing mentors, but also by my determination and ability to push forward. My most important lesson of all is that you must take the wheel to navigate to unknown places, because only then you will learn to push yourself to limits. Remember that while you are not always selected or given opportunities you'd like; you should not wait for someone else to open a door for you. You can make things happen yourself.

REFLECT AND RISE

As you read through my story, I hope that you feel inspired to create your own path. Here's what I want you to keep in mind:

1. Don't be afraid to ask for opportunities. The worst thing they can say is "no."

2. Seek what you want and do not let others stop you. Write your own proposals detailing your accomplishments, and be persistent because you deserve it.

3. Titles are just words. Don't get caught up in the illusion that titles dictate accomplishments. It is what you do with your job that matters.

4. Build meaningful connections and be approachable. Then others can connect with you authentically.

BIOGRAPHY

Luz was born in the Dominican Republic, raised in New York, and is now a proud mother to two beautiful daughters. She describes her experiences and life transitions as ever-evolving.

Starting at a very young age, Luz developed a passion and drive to make a difference in her community. Her need to evolve and continue to learn about her roots led her to join college organizations where she gained leadership skills and community involvement. Luz earned a sociology degree and a master's degree at Binghamton University.

Luz has spent the last eight years as a business partner at a Fortune 200 Company specializing in IT services and solutions. Her job consists of partnering with business leaders to oversee the implementation of strategic initiatives and corporate policy practices and assisting with implementing solutions to meet talent goals. Throughout the years, Luz has developed a deep passion for the human resources field, and especially enjoys coaching and developing people. Her business goal is to always accept new challenges in efforts to expand her business acumen and to attain well-rounded experiences to start a future consulting business in HR.

Luz Perez

Manager, HRBP

Years in HR: 14

luzhpichardo@gmail.com

Linkedin.com/in/luzhperez.

MY JOURNEY HOME

BY PAMELA CARMEN BURGA

"Dale Ganas."

As I opened the door to my apartment, rolled in my carry-on luggage and collapsed against the cool wall of the hallway entrance, I sighed. My building had bright pink, Greek architecture with Prometheus prominently on display in the front. It was a beachfront property, four hundred feet from the sands of Playa del Rey with a spectacular rooftop overseeing the California coastline. Just hours before, I had delivered a TEDx Talk to a room full of senior executives on the executive floor of a Fortune 10 company headquartered in Dallas.

I had been selected out of one hundred and thirty applications to present at this prestigious event, which was filmed for broadcast available to over three hundred thousand employees. I'll never forget that moment, as I sat on the floor pondering, "How did I get here?"

AN EDUCATION IN EDUCATION

Statistically, I shouldn't have been there nor had many of my life experiences to date. Playa del Rey is far away from my hometown of Pomona, California, where, according to the U.S. Census Bureau, the per capita income is about half the state's average; nearly a quarter of children live in poverty; youth struggle in school and drop out; more than thirty percent of adults don't have a high school degree; only seventeen percent have college degrees; and violent crime is well over the national average.

As a first-generation American of Mexican-Peruvian descent, this was the lens through which I saw the world as a child and I believed that most people in America lived like I did — speaking Spanish with profoundly loving parents, having a best friend who lived in a neighbor's garage with her single mom and three siblings, and using tickets instead of money to pay for school lunches. I believed that this was the norm. It wasn't until I transferred to a neighboring school district that I realized my norm was actually the proverbial "other side of the tracks." In my case, it was just ten minutes away from my previous school on the other side of the I-10 freeway.

The cars in this blue-ribbon school's parking lot were mainly new BMWs and Jettas, and the college acceptance rate was more than eighty percent. I was the only Latina in most of my AP classes. It was also the first time that I hid the ticket for my school lunches, out of shame.

Although I didn't know it then, my high school experience exposed me for the first time to the concept of educational inequality. After graduation, I essentially received a full ride to a prestigious, local liberal arts school, because my mother wouldn't let me apply out of state. While reading education author Jonathan Kozol's work for one of my sociology classes, it became clear that my experiences were not isolated. Educational inequity was a deeply-rooted, systemic problem in our country.

Since that experience, I have felt responsibility to change things and to level the playing field for the underrepresented, like my friends and me. I took action and committed to making upward mobility the norm. Little did I know I was in for quite the adventure.

FEARLESS CURIOSITY

In an essay titled "Dear Woke Brown Girl," published in The Huffington Post, Prisca Dorcas Mojica Rodriguez wrote, "You are going places that no one in your family has ever been and you are fearful of your fearlessness." It makes me emotional every time I read it.

I was privileged to have a family that always encouraged me to pursue my dreams and defy socially-constructed gender limitations. In discussions about professional dreams, they would say things like, *"Dale ganas!"* which meant if you're going to do something, "do it with heart!" But they also wanted me to fit in the box of a traditional, well-adjusted Latina daughter. Sometimes I think they would have been happier if I had done what most of my friends and family did—married young and gave their parents some grandchildren.

But I'm different.

I have always raised my hand to unexpected, outside-of-the-norm opportunities. As a young adult, I studied abroad in both Italy and Cuba, and I traveled to more than twenty countries. Singing is my passion, and I have performed at the Disney Concert Hall and the Lincoln Center. During stints in working for political campaigns, I met Joe Biden, Kamala Harris, Hilary Clinton, and Barack Obama. I even once drove Michelle Obama and her daughters around southern California for a day during Obama's first campaign.

I have been to Burning Man twice, moderated panels in front of thousands, spoken on a panel alongside HR thought leader Laszlo Bock, former Google chief people officer, and my name is floating in outer space on a placard attached to the red Tesla sports car that Elon Musk launched into orbit in 2018. I did all of this while advancing my career and committing to social causes.

From an outsider looking in, it may seem that my

career journey makes sense. I started with work in social impact, then pursued HR, and now work in Diversity and Inclusion (D&I), blending the two. Brilliant. But in reality, for the longest time, my non-linear path was a source of insecurity.

In a recent podcast, Elizabeth Gilbert advised about following your curiosity instead of your passion. For those who don't have a singular passion but instead have many interests, following your curiosity "will keep you pleasantly distracted while life sorts itself out... Before you even realize what's happening, it may have led you safely all the way home." This was my experience. My drive to help underrepresented groups launched my career, and while I have worked in different positions and industries, this north star was always present.

After college, I moved to New York City, without knowing anybody, to fight for educational equality and to teach kindergarten in the Bronx through Teach For America. After completing my tenure, I returned to Los Angeles and worked on political campaigns and education policy for the second largest district in the country. I already had my M.S. in Education, but after seeing that most local, non-profit leaders were MBA-holding white men, I realized that if I wanted to have a bigger impact, I should have a business degree too.

As the first college graduate in the family, I had no

one close to ask for advice about grad school, much less business school. That was until I discovered programs dedicated to increasing diversity in business schools. The Management Leadership for Tomorrow (MLT), Riordan Fellows, and Consortium programs led me to a full ride at a top twenty business school in Los Angeles, where I was the only American Latina in my class of 220 students.

In business school, I fell in love with my organizational behavior class and learned about the possibilities of a career in HR. Karen Williams, my advisor and one of my life mentors, coached me on how to interview as a career switcher. This helped me land an internship at a Fortune 5 healthcare company that summer. To my surprise, I was the only underrepresented intern out of a cohort of twenty-five.

After graduating, I participated in a HR leadership rotation program and left a comfortable job with a promotion path to join a company intent on colonizing Mars. While working in HR at this aerospace company, I organized a mentoring program for female engineers that saw great success. D&I work felt rewarding, and I realized then that I wanted to follow that curiosity full time.

CHANGE AND CHOICE

The very next day, I applied for a D&I role in live music entertainment. I threw my hat in the ring, without high expectations, and succeeded in the interview process. In that role, I launched the Latinx Employee Resource Group across the country and enlisted new leaders and executive sponsors to champion group efforts. Things were trending upwards when COVID -19 hit the industry like the iceberg hit the Titanic.

Waves of furloughs crashed down every couple of weeks, but the protests following George Floyd's death elevated the need for D&I strategies across corporate America. Before I knew it, I was recruited to work for one of the edgiest, sustainable energy companies in the world. I was excited about my new job and ready to put the pedal to the metal, one hundred and ten percent, but my world was about to change yet again.

Since I no longer had to commute to LA, I moved back in with my eighty-one and ninety-one year-old parents in Pomona to help them. The same night that I returned, my beloved, older brother called from an emergency room. He had been preliminary diagnosed with pancreatic cancer. We only had our nuclear family, so I knew it would be up to me to step up and steer the ship.

The following month, I ran on pure adrenaline. I was making appointments, dealing with hospital and insurance bureaucracy, learning about stage four pancreatic cancer, and breaking the news to my elderly parents. Just weeks into my new job, I was taking work conference calls next to my brother during his first round of chemotherapy in the middle of a pandemic.

I struggled with having to relax my pedal-to-metal mentality and instead ask for help and lean on my new teammates. And when I finally got my courageous brother into a steady place and there was some cadence to his chemo treatment, unfamiliar feelings started to hit me. It felt like whiplash. As denial and numbness subsided about this new normal, deep sadness and anxiety set in.

I don't always know what to do with these feelings. I'm still living this. I wrote part of this chapter in the emergency room, waiting with my brother to be seen because of a complication. Later, I had to take my dad to the hospital for an infection, then watch over my mom for her blood pressure— all in the middle of COVID-19 stay-at-home orders, a racial and political climate war, and immense wildfires just miles away.

Back to Pomona from Playa del Rey, I'm now typing work emails and this essay at the very same wooden desk where I did high school homework. I take walks by my old elementary school, my old church, and my aunt's house pondering the metaphorical essence of finding myself exactly where I started. There have been moments in my life where I've applied lots of pressure on myself to achieve, sometimes to an unhealthy degree. But in these heightened moments, where I'm forced to assess what's important, one life lesson continues to speak to me: my worth does not depend on my job, college, grades, status, or even traditional expectations. I know who I am.

As someone who has sprinted and leapt through her journey, it's been hard adjusting instead to a marathon pace. For you over-achievers who may be experiencing setbacks, moments of doubt or deep despair, diversions from your plans, loss of control while the earth is shattering around you—through a pandemic or otherwise—I leave you with one of my hardest lessons this year: stay focused on putting one foot in front of the other and give yourself some grace. Just remember to do it with heart.

REFLECT AND RISE

In these challenging times, I leave you with keys to success that have served me well:

- **Boundaries.** During a recent interview, Dr. Brené Brown discussed research she conducted with the most compassionate people in the world (e.g. monks). Their common trait? Boundaries of steel. "Compassionate people say no when they need to, and when they say yes, they mean it. Their boundaries keep them out of resentment."

- **Personal Board of Directors.** Building a network is especially important if you are also a first-generation college student who cannot easily rely on uncles, aunts, and neighbors to easily advise you on the unwritten rules at different stages of upward mobility, from interviewing for a college internship to salary negotiations for a senior role. Don't forget to include peers who may have different areas of expertise than you, to mock interview with and remind you, in moments of doubt, the value you bring the table.

- **Imposter Syndrome.** It's a real, widespread phenomenon that nobody talks about for fear of being found out. When it sneaks in, remember these (summarized) words from Marianne Williamson: "Our deepest fear is not that we are inadequate. Our deepest fear is that we are powerful beyond measure. We ask ourselves, 'Who am I to be brilliant, gorgeous, talented, fabulous?' Actually, who are you not to be? You are a child of God. Playing small does not serve the world. And as we let our own light shine, we unconsciously give other people permission to do the same."

BIOGRAPHY

With more than fifteen years of effectively leveraging strong interpersonal and analytical skills to coach and advise executives and diverse stakeholders, Pamela Burga has driven individual and team performance in a variety of industries, including tech, government, entertainment, education, aerospace, and healthcare.

Pamela works on Diversity, Equity, & Inclusion (DEI) at Tesla and leads the enterprise DEI talent development strategy. Prior to Tesla, Pamela held leadership roles in D&I, compensation, talent attraction, and as an HR business partner at SpaceX, Live Nation Entertainment, McKesson, DIRECTV Latin America, and AT&T.

While earning her MBA from the University of Southern California (USC) Marshall School of Business, Pamela was recognized with awards and fellowships from The Consortium for Graduate Study in Management, Management Leadership for Tomorrow (MLT), Nestlé, The East Los Angeles Community Union (TELACU), and the USC Latino Alumni Association. She also served as senior policy director for the LA Unified School District (LAUSD) Board of Education and on staff for former Los Angeles Mayor Antonio Villaraigosa.

While earning her M.S. in Education at Pace University, Pamela taught kindergarten in the Bronx, NY through Teach For America. She has a B.A. in Public

Policy Analysis/Politics and a minor in classical voice from Pomona College.

Pamela Burga

Diversity & Inclusion Leader

Years in HR: 6

Burgaconsulting@gmail.com

LinkedIn.com/in/pamelaburga

BY MERCEDES JAIME

"If we can't take the time to invest in ourselves, how will we discover what we value?"

My grandfather used to say, *"No hay mal que por bien no venga,"* which means when something bad happens, something good comes out of it. It's absolutely true! There are blessings in disguise.

If we trace back the past failures, disappointments, and significant emotional events in our lives, it always comes back as an evolution and an opportunity for us to make changes, to learn, and retool! It is a growth opportunity that we must hone to change our view from "why me?" to "what is this trying to teach me?"

We have all experienced significantly emotional events in our lives. It's okay to honor the hurt and disappointments and to give ourselves time to grieve the person, relationship, or circumstance that changed

159

our lives. However, we must find the ability to look at our situation through a different lens and explore what the situation is trying to teach us. How can I evolve and learn from this loss or failure? Ask yourself the most important question — do I love this and does it make me happy?

INTENTIONAL LIVING

I have learned that love is the most powerful feeling in the world. It overcomes every good and bad feeling. When we are faced with a bad situation or a difficult person, it is a challenge to choose to adjust the lens and transform the negative into a positive. It takes much practice to change our perception of a person or situation and learn to love and evolve as an individual. Before we take the leap of change, we first need to invest in ourselves and do a self-assessment. We need to identify our values, roles, and expectations.

Why is this self-investment necessary? If we can't take the time to invest in ourselves, how will we discover what we value, our role in life, and what we expect of ourselves? We tend to make time to research about people, places, and items of interest but when was the last time you looked at yourself and your daily life, and asked why you are doing what you are doing? Why am I working for this organization? Why am I invested in this relationship?

The truth is that we rarely think about "why" we do

the things that we do. We settle into the routine of our daily habitual behavior and we rarely act intentionally. What does it mean to be intentional and live in the moment? I heard somewhere that when we are in the shower, we are not actually in the shower. Instead we are doing other things like planning our day, adding to our mental grocery list, or having an imaginary conversation. We never just enjoy the shower or bath and take the time to feel the water run over our bodies to release the tension and stress from our daily lives. We don't take the time to nurture our bodies and honor that time to clean, rejuvenate, and rehabilitate our body, mind, and soul. Let's start by devoting time daily in our morning to bathe or shower intentionally.

My belief is that on a good day or a bad day, you still have your morning routine. I wake up before my alarm, I set a timer on my nightstand to allow myself time to relax, stretch, and sometimes say a prayer or meditation as I'm thankful for another day. Then I get up, make my bed, change into my bathing suit, and plan out my day and enjoy breakfast, either before or after my morning swim.

The night before, I get my gym bag ready and select my attire and accessories for the following day. Why is this important? It's important to me because I want to feel comfortable in my attire to take on my day!

My daily bliss is an hour in the pool. My morning

swim is the first thing on my calendar and very few things come before this VIP appointment. It's my time alone and away from the world. It is the time that I dedicate to my mind, body, and soul. Every night I look forward to my morning swim. Sometimes, I double my personal time in the evening to help wrap up the day. Your bliss may be lifting weights, knitting, reading, walking, or running. Whatever your bliss, prioritize it into your daily schedule. I discovered my love for swimming seven years ago when I was rehabilitating from a tragic car accident that marked a significant emotional event in my life.

POWER FROM PAIN

On the afternoon of May 20, 2013, my parents and I were celebrating with my middle daughter after she had received her driver's license. My parents were visiting from out of state and were beaming with pride for their granddaughter. Then in an instant, our lives changed. While driving home, our vehicle was cut off and T-boned by a semi-trailer. My mother died immediately upon impact, and both my father and I were seriously injured. I was diagnosed with a brain injury, broken clavicle, and broken ribs. My father suffered broken ribs and a shoulder injury. Miraculously, my daughter walked away with a few cuts and bruises.

Many months of physical therapy, cognitive rehabilitation,

and significant emotional events followed. It was a very long process but in the midst of our blessing in disguise, I discovered my love for swimming. My daily commitment was to be in the water for an hour and that's what kept me going.

As a supplier diversity professional, I know that it takes time, persuasion, and creativity to connect small businesses and stakeholders of large corporations with opportunities. I loved my work, devoting a lot of time, focus, and positivity to it. After my rehabilitation, I returned to work just as my employer was going through an organizational transition which affected my team. I became disturbed to learn that some of the new leadership didn't prioritize the business practice of diversity and inclusion. I also felt that there were unwritten rules in the new corporate culture that excluded me and a hierarchy of who could talk to who. As a Latina, I didn't always feel that I could bring my whole self to work. I didn't feel listened to or valued. Since I have extensive experience having grown up in the grocery business and because I value myself, I bristled at those rules.

New challenges were also surfacing at home. My divorce finalized in 2015. An important lesson for me was that divorce does not equal fairness. As professional women, we need to understand that as we empower ourselves to be financially independent, we may also carry the burden of giving up more or being prepared to support our ex's lifestyle as a result of being the major income earner.

FAMILY TOGETHERNESS

In 2017, after more than thirty years in business, my exit strategy from corporate America included paying off my vehicle and all credit card debt, prepaying six months on my mortgage and utility bills, and revising my budget so that I could invest and save more money.

I also scheduled a professional financial planning session with my daughters. "Your mother has decided to give you an equal sum of money for you to start investing in your future," the financial planner told them. "I will be your financial planner. You are never to ask your mother for another dime because this is for your financial future." I remember how stunned their little faces were. It was as if I gave a kid a toy that they could only see and not touch.

Six months later, I launched my own business to help companies build a supplier diversity program. By working with many companies, I am now spreading the diversity and inclusion message to a wider audience than I did in the past.

In June of 2017, to celebrate a birthday milestone, I chose Cuba as the destination for my first cruise. It was a lifelong dream to visit the island and to experience the culture and historical sites. What a life changing experience to just unplug from life with no telephone, internet, news, stress, or children! It was an absolute removal from the daily routine allowing me to be and live in the moment. Nine days of pure bliss!

In June of 2018, my oldest daughter was married at our home. Although it was a very happy time, it was also extremely stressful. Two weeks before the wedding, my middle daughter was diagnosed with cancer. It was another significant emotional event and a blessing in disguise for our family. My eldest wanted to cancel her wedding. As a family, we decided to move forward with the wedding plans before the effect of my middle daughter's chemotherapy became too obvious. She had just turned twenty-one.

It took nine months, two biopsies, over a dozen doctors, and a lot of prayers after a misdiagnosed and failed treatment. After getting a second opinion, doctors discovered that she had stage two Hodgkin's lymphoma. I had a breakdown. I felt helpless, but watching my daughter's inner strength gave me the power to move forward. I believe in the power of attraction and became very intentional in asking, believing, and receiving a cancer-free daughter by Christmas of 2018.

In June of 2019, my youngest daughter and I traveled to Europe, visiting Switzerland, Germany, and Austria. It was a mother-daughter high school graduation trip with three other mother-daughter friends. My middle daughter, now cancer-free, also graduated from university in December of 2019. It was a great milestone and an opportunity for a family celebration.

In 2020, COVID-19 became another significant emotional event and a blessing in disguise. It has been a full house since all three of my daughters have moved back home. We have had many family quarantine dinners, family movie nights, and too close for comfort time while social distancing from the world of our extended family and friends.

Today, I am happy to report that my oldest daughter and her husband purchased their first home and welcomed their first baby in April. My middle daughter has started a business and is expecting a baby in Spring 2021. My youngest daughter is a sophomore in college. And I am looking forward to this new life chapter as an empty nester.

REFLECT AND RISE

My advice to supplier diversity professionals revolves around the way we should approach work and life.

- **Love the work that you do daily.** It makes a difference in the way you view your role.
- **Understand the corporate culture and decide if it**

aligns with your values, roles, and expectations. Have an exit strategy prepared if the corporate value system does not align with yours.

- **Always return phone calls and answer emails.** Manage supplier's expectations well because it could be a dangerous arena for a small company to do business with large corporations. Hidden fees, complex policies, and the lack of understanding on how to conduct business could lead to painful lessons.

- **Learn to stay focused and positive because you'll always get the door slammed in your face due to the myths of corporate America.** It takes time, persuasion, and creativity to connect a small business with a corporation's stakeholder and create an opportunity for a new product or service.

- **A successful supplier diversity program needs advocates at all organizational levels.** Corporate warriors must be willing to advocate, mentor, and teach in order to help transform an organization's supply chain to mirror their customer base.

BIOGRAPHY

Mercedes E. Jaime is founder and CEO of Enter Entra, LLC. As a supplier and D&I professional, she is a power-connector with more than thirty years of experience strategizing, establishing, and managing B2B relationships. Her passion and expertise have resulted in improved access by leveraging successful business practices to ensure equitable opportunities and growth for organizations of all sizes. Mercedes is an active leader in numerous national and international organizations that represent and support the causes of women, minorities, LGBT, veteran, and diverse business entrepreneurs. Due to Mercedes' contributions to the field of supplier diversity, she has been honored with awards such as the "America's Top 100 Leaders in Corporate Supplier Diversity" by Women's Enterprise USA in 2014, "Diversity in Business Award 2015" by *Minneapolis/St. Paul Business Journal,* and the "Top 25 Women in Power Impacting Diversity" by *DiversityPlus* Magazine in 2015. She also received the National Association Women Business Owners (NAWBO) Advocate Award in 2019.

Mercedes is committed to a strategic procurement process that meets the diverse needs of customers and retailer businesses. Her deep desire to support all minorities, while fostering a sense of belonging and power, is an integral part of her D&I goals.

Mercedes Jaime

Supplier Diversity Professional

Years in HR: 12

mercedes.e.jaime@gmail.com

Linkedin.com/in/mercedes-e-jaime/

CHUTES AND LADDERS

BY KARINA PRO

"No matter what, you have to keep rolling that dice to get to that finish line."

It takes courage, will, and perseverance to live your life. We all have varying degrees of courage. For some, it is buried deep in our hearts and psyches. For others, it is a bright light that guides you through every step. But, for all of us, finding courage, will, and perseverance can be a choice we make every day — often in the quietest of ways. Simply getting up every day and putting one foot in front of the other is an act of immense courage, will, and perseverance. Life is like the board game of Chutes and Ladders. You roll the dice and move to the first square.

SQUARE ONE

My first roll of the dice and step onto the first square on the board game started when both of my parents emigrated from Michoacán, Mexico in the early eighties. They walked for days upon days through the deserts of Mexico. We finally arrived at one the Texas borders and were detained by the immigration authorities. We were released into the custody of my American aunt, Hope Pino.

We had to report to immigration for years on a periodic basis, and I remember at age five being asked what school I was going to, who my teacher was, and what subjects I liked. Going to those meetings made me nervous and anxious. I was afraid that the officer would put my parents and me back in jail.

I grew up in Little Village, a predominantly Latino community in Chicago, Illinois, which felt like "home." The people there didn't speak English and children suddenly became translators for their parents and neighbors. As I grew, I experienced the injustice towards the Latino community firsthand. Many were getting arrested without hearing their rights read to them or coerced into signing documents without giving full consent or having full knowledge of what they were signing. Innocent community members were being arrested without due process. This is the moment where I realized that I wanted to become an attorney.

As a child, you are taught to have a plan and to do certain things to get to your goal. What they don't tell you about is all the obstacles and challenges that you will encounter to get to that goal. There were numerous challenges and obstacles that I encountered to reach my dream of becoming an attorney. My first obstacle was my parents. To get to law school you must first graduate from high school, then graduate from a university but I was expected to find a job and help support the family. There was no way that my family could afford to send me to college.

This changed for me when I met my high school teacher, Ms. Imelda Vega, who taught world studies at Kelly High School. She was the first educated Latina who truly pushed me to do more and reach for my dreams. She told me that I too could attend college. I told her that my parents only expected me to graduate from high school and that they couldn't afford college. She encouraged me to do better and to apply to universities. She began giving me scholarship applications, informational material on colleges within the city, and pointers on writing my personal statement. She even kept an eye on me to keep me out of trouble.

As you know, most kids can easily drift away with the wrong crowds in high school. I couldn't have, though. Ms. Vega was always around to keep me in check. Ms. Vega was an alumna of the University of Illinois at Urbana-Champaign, and she took me on a personal tour of the campus. She made sure that I knew the history of the original La Casa. La Casa is a resource, an advocate, and a safe space for all students, inclusive of differing nationalities, citizenship, or immigrant status. This was the place to be. It was our home away from home.

I applied to the University of Illinois and was beyond happy to be accepted. The emotion opening up that letter overtook my inner soul. It was becoming very real. I, a native of Mexico, brought to the U.S. to have a better life, was about to experience the "American dream." I made it into one of the best colleges in the state of Illinois. I was floating on cloud nine.

Then, I was brought down to the living reality of wondering how I was going to afford college. I suddenly felt a big hole in my stomach. My parents didn't have the money to send me to college. Ms. Vega responded with, "Where there's a will there's a way." I told my father that I had been accepted to U of I. I expected him to be happy for me, but I didn't get the response I was hoping for. Instead, he told me that I could not leave my house unless I was married.

I was shocked to hear him say this to me. I thought he should be proud and happy to know that I was accepted into a good university. His sacrifices and hard work for his children to have better lives and opportunities was finally paying off!

I now had the challenge of overcoming the Mexican traditions and the difference in gender roles. Mexican daughters were to marry before leaving their homes; otherwise they must remain and take care of their parents. If they're the oldest, they must also take care of their siblings. As a family member, you wouldn't dare challenge the decision of the leader of the house.

I had no choice but to go against my father's decision that I must wed before leaving the family home. I accepted the offer and continued with the process of becoming a Fighting Illini. My father did eventually come around and he started investigating the school by asking his American friends. They must have spoken very well of U of I. He started bragging to other family members that I was to go to "El U of I."

This was quite a new adventure for my parents. They were used to always having the family in one house, and now, I was going off to college. I remember arriving at my dorm and my father saw the room that I would be sharing with another roommate. He asked if my roommate was another girl and said he would call to check up on me and make sure I wasn't having boys in the room.

SQUARE TWO

At this point I was rolling the dice and kept moving forward one square to the next. I was enjoying college life. My next roll of the dice brought me down the chute. In my third year of college, my father was deported to Mexico. This was devastating for my family, at a time when deportations were starting to rise again. If you were at the wrong place at the wrong time, and you were arrested as a permanent resident, you were going to be questioned and deported. Any criminal offense, even the smallest infraction or occurrence, could be used against you in the justice system.

My father happened to be in the wrong place at the wrong time. For many years, in the traditional Mexican family, the father was the leader of the house. He was the breadwinner and also the person who kept the family together. I now became the one to financially support my family and hold them together.

This was the most challenging time of my life. I had to work three jobs while taking eighteen hours of classes at U of I. I also had to drive back and forth from Champaign, Illinois to Chicago three times a week to meet with my father's attorney and run a retail business in the Pilsen area, as well as emotionally support my mother and siblings. This was the lowest point of my life and I went into a state of depression. It was my biggest test.

How could I continue? I had to keep going. I had to be the one to stay strong. My family needed someone to be strong and hold them together. They were torn apart by the injustices of our judicial system. From two hours away, I continued to try to take care of my siblings and my mother, who spoke very little English. I thought about dropping out of college at one point, but I couldn't do that. I had worked too hard to get there. Plus, I could hear my father say, "I didn't raise a quitter." I had to make it work.

THE FINISH LINE

After graduation, I had no energy to take care of anyone else or continue on with law school. My goal to go to law school was postponed for ten years. I moved to Tampa, Florida and started to work as a loan processor with Countrywide Home loans. For a while, all was going well. I was again moving onto another square, and another, until I reached a chute. During the housing crisis in 2008, I lost my job in the mortgage industry. I also lost everything that I had built and found myself with a clean slate to move on. This was my opportunity to return to law school.

I started applying to law schools and was accepted to one in Michigan. One week after receiving the acceptance letter, I found out that I was expecting my second child. There was no turning back and I prepared to go to law school. I started classes when my son was only one week old. This was the next challenge that I would endure. How do you make it through law school with an infant?

"No big deal!" I said. "I had already juggled my

father's case, kept my mom from committing suicide, ran our business, sold my father's business, and finished college. I got this!" I graduated law school in 2014. Before graduation, I completed an internship as a law clerk at Metropolitan Family Services in Chicago. During my internship, I was asked by the vice president of human resources/general counsel to help the human resources team. This was my entrance into the world of human resources.

I was involved with employee relations and I was given the opportunity to assist with establishing strong working relationships between the employee and employer. I also worked on projects to create a more diversified workforce. It was fascinating to respond to employee complaints and grievances. I used my legal background and provided neutral guidance to both parties.

After graduation, I was hired onto the HR team. This was not part of my plan. My plan for thirty years of my life was to become an attorney. Now, I have been in human resources for over seven years and I enjoy every minute of it. Life doesn't always follow your plan.

What I've learned from these obstacles and challenges is that you have to embrace them. Every challenge and obstacle that happens in your life happens for a reason. Life is like the game of Chutes and Ladders. You roll the dice and walk, run, skip or hop onto the next square. You may go up a ladder or slide right down that chute. No matter what, you have to keep rolling that dice to get to that finish line. You must not give up. Your courage, will, and perseverance will be tested as well as your psyche. I can guarantee if you fast forward twenty years into the future, you will realize that every challenge or obstacle you encountered prepared you for life!

REFLECT AND RISE

Reflect on your life and the challenge you have faced.

1. Where can I find resources to inspire me and to fuel my will and perseverance?

2. Who do I want my mentor to be for my personal and professional life?

3. What things ground me and refuel me?

4. Think about a challenge or obstacle in your life. What is this challenge or obstacle trying to teach or what can you learn from it? Is it a teachable moment?

BIOGRAPHY

Karina Pro is the senior director of human resources at Children's Home & Aid. She has seven years of experience working alongside the leadership and executive team of a nonprofit agency.

Karina received her Juris Doctorate from Western Michigan Thomas Cooley Law School. She now specializes in employment law and is responsible for educating employees on how to strengthen the employer-employee relationship through identifying and resolving workplace issues. Karina is a powerful force in the workplace and uses her positive attitude and tireless energy to encourage others to work hard and succeed.

Karina is inspired daily by her two sons. In her free time, she likes to hike, garden, and watch foreign movies.

Karina Pro

Sr. Director of Human Resources

Years in HR: 8

Karinapro7@gmail.com

Linkedin.com/in/karina-pro-0aa119118

OVERCOMING OBSTACLES: THE PATH OF AN HR RISING STAR

BY SONYA LAMAS

"Don't forget to pause and take care of yourself and those around you."

I am a thirty-nine -years "young" Latina and proud mother of a twenty-five-year-old aspiring actor. Yes, if you do the math correctly, you will learn I was a teen mother. In fact, I was fourteen years old when I had my son, Daniel.

I am the second oldest of six and we are the first generation to come to the U.S. My parents brought us back to the states when I was six years old and did not speak a lick of English. I found myself trying to fit in while learning the language. I always loved school, excelled in math, and thought I wanted to be a lawyer, someone who would help people like my parents. They are hard-working people who would give up their entire life to pursue the American Dream for their kids.

MOTHERHOOD AT 14

When my parents found out I was "dating," I was asked to leave the house and be with my boyfriend at the age of fourteen. It was then my plans of becoming a lawyer--my dreams, my desires, and how I would accomplish them--changed drastically.

I finished middle school with honors and five months pregnant. I remember that my teachers had to get a doctor's clearance for me to be allowed to take the famous East Coast trip that I had won in a scholarship competition.

I was blessed to have a healthy pregnancy and to deliver my baby at the beginning of high school. It was an exciting time for most teenagers, and even though I was a mother, a freshman in high school, and a homemaker, I never gave up on school. During my sophomore year, I found a high school where I could take Daniel with me and he would stay in the infant lab while I went to class.

After verbal and physical abuse by the father of my child, I decided to leave him. This meant figuring out how to provide for my two- year-old son and keeping a roof over our heads. Not only did I waitress on the weekends to make ends meet, but I found myself receiving public aid, and vowed not to stay in the system.

FOR THE LOVE OF THE GAME

My dad played soccer when he was young, and I grew a passion for the sport in order to make him proud and lessen his disappointment in me. As a full-time mom, a full-time high school student, and part-time waitress, I decided I would try out for soccer and relieve all my stress on the soccer field.

I had never played soccer but had an idea of the game rules from watching the sport with my dad on television on Sundays. At the tryout, I was on that damn field chasing every single ball kicked to me. I am sure Mr. Olmsted, my soccer coach, saw my desire, resilience, determination, and eagerness to join the team. Despite my lack of soccer skills, he gave me a spot.

By the end of my high school years, I finished as a triathlete, having participated in soccer, volleyball, and track. I fell in love with how sports kept me grounded, despite all the life challenges, and it made me feel part of something bigger than myself while celebrating our losses and victories. I realized then that no matter how big or small you may be, you are only as good as your team.

After high school I went to community college and declined an invitation to play soccer for a local college because of the travel requirements. Who would watch Daniel while I followed my love for the sport? So, I found an all-women's, local soccer league and was on the soccer field every Sunday, rain or shine, hungover, injured, or tired, supporting my team because I could never let them down.

CLIMBING THE CORPORATE LADDER

Daniel and I moved to Norwich, Connecticut, where I landed a temporary job as an office coordinator for a staffing agency. It was supposed to be seasonal position, but I was the only Spanish-speaking person in the office, so they turned it into a permanent one.

Despite a lack of experience, I was fulfilled because I felt passionate about what I was doing. I was helping people find jobs, but the best part was helping Latinx find jobs. After a few years, Daniel and I moved back to San Diego where I accepted a position as human resources coordinator for a hotel and attended San Diego State University (SDSU).

I quickly fell in love with the job and those I worked with, but most importantly, who I was becoming--a resource to many colleagues who often felt more comfortable talking to me about work-related challenges than with their own managers. Just when I felt ready for more responsibility, my job was eliminated from the economic downturn.

My world had flipped upside down and soon after, I quit school. I had a teenager who ate as if it was our last day on earth, and I needed to find a job. I applied for several positions until I met the human resource director of the largest hotel in San Diego, who was looking for a Spanish-speaking employment manager to join his team. Eight interviews later, I accepted a pilot area recruiter role for two Hyatt hotels, Andaz San Diego and Grand Hyatt San Diego.

Not only did I have to prove myself, but I had to make sure the pilot was successful, all while parenting a fourteen-year-old son. Three years later, I absorbed a third hotel and trained other area recruiters until I accepted a promotion to learning and development manager.

Rob Spooner, the human resources director, quickly became my mentor and my biggest supporter, not only professionally, but personally as well. "When are you going back to school, Sonya?" he would often ask. I remember avoiding his office because I was running out of excuses. After several months in that role, I accepted a promotion to area learning and development manager for five hotels in San Diego.

BACK TO SCHOOL

It was then I asked myself, "How come I am not going back to school?" All I could remember was how scared I was to fail. Then, Rob asked me again. This time I went to get my transcripts at SDSU. Once I was in my car, envelope in hand, I opened it and cried. I would have to work a little harder to build up my GPA if I wanted to reapply to SDSU again. I talked to Daniel about it, and why I was afraid. I always wanted to go back to school--to make myself, my son, and my family proud of me. Even more, I wanted to go back and finish so I would not be a statistic--Latina, teen mom, and a college dropout.

A week later, I walked into the house where Daniel was waiting for me with a backpack that he had purchased and stocked for me with school supplies. He handed me a card with a baby's hand holding his mother's hand on the front. It said, "You have been talking about going back to school for a long time and I want you to do it." He said how proud he was of my hard work and everything I had done for both of us.

I cried and hugged him because I knew there was no turning back. Not long after, I sat in my first class with a huge knot in my throat. I was scared and questioned my purpose. Then I remembered Daniel's card and Rob's support. I soon met other students with similar goals and came back to class twice a week to complete my B.S. in Business Management.

Six months after returning to school, Hyatt called, asking if I would be interested in returning to the recruiting team to launch another pilot. This time I would become director of talent acquisition and recruit for eleven Hyatt Hotels in California and Nevada.

I always knew I was the crazy and daring one in my family, and this confirmed it. Now I was responsible for the structure and implementation of recruiting strategies for eleven hotels while continuing to attend night classes twice a week. In early 2018, while in that role, I was awarded the Association of Latino Professionals For America's Most Powerful Latina in Hyatt Rising Star.

In May 2018, I finally accomplished my goal and walked on stage to receive my degree in the presence of my family. Soon after, Daniel moved to New York to attend acting school and fight for his dream of becoming an actor.

I became lonely, confused, sad, and lost, as if someone had ripped off the right side of my body. I was missing my son. He was my reason to fight for more in life, to keep wanting to be a better mother, daughter, sister, and colleague, and now he was so far away.

I missed being around other people, so I took a new job as assistant director of human resources in Lake Tahoe and was the acting human resources director for the first four months. I moved from city where it was a year-round seventy-five-degrees to a freezing small town where the winter was brutal, lonely, and sometimes dangerous, especially for a single woman who had no idea how to drive in four feet of snow if the street had not been plowed. However, this relocation was definitely a career move to become director of human resources. I survived twenty feet of snow during my first and only winter, and just as the snow was starting to melt away, I escaped to become the colleague experience director at Hyatt Regency Santa Clara where I remain in warmer temperatures.

While it is important to follow your career and relocate in search of the next promotion, it's also important to balance life with what is most important for you at that time. Our lives, our kids, and our priorities will change, so don't forget to pause and take care of yourself and those around you.

I currently have the job I wanted, and I enjoy it just as much as I had imagined, but I never thought I would be alone in a city without my family around. My goal now is to make my way back home, and while others may think they know what the best move for me should be, I know now that I will have the final say.

REFLECT AND RISE

In my journey I have learned many lessons. I would like to share them with you.

- **No one knows it all.** Therefore, build a network of colleagues and friends so that you can help each other when the phone rings.

- **Share the knowledge and give credit where credit is due.** People will be more inclined to assist you when the recognition is shared.

- **Bring value your HR team.** Colleagues often think HR is the fun department and all we do is plan parties and celebrations. We can, and should, but we do so much more.

- **Be human too.** Share your personal story so that colleagues know you too have feelings and will make mistakes like all humans do. This will help build trust.

BIOGRAPHY

Sonya Lamas is a San Diego native who has also lived in Norwich, Connecticut, and northern California. She began her career in human resources for Starwood Hotels in 2007.

In 2010, Sonya joined Hyatt as one of the first area recruiters, and in ten years piloted two human resources roles. She also led a team and managed the recruiting cycle for eleven hotels before joining the Hyatt Regency Lake Tahoe in 2018. While there, she played a vital role in the department as a leader, and encouraged a culture of understanding, care, and fun. She is currently the colleague experience director at Hyatt Regency Santa Clara.

Sonya attended San Diego State University and the University of Phoenix where she completed her B.S. in Business Management. She played soccer for seventeen years, and flag football for four years. Sonya has been a Stay Fit@Hyatt co-captain for the National Multiple Sclerosis Society for the past eight years, biking one hundred miles to raise money and bring awareness to MS.

Her son in New York is her pride and joy. When not playing or watching a sport, Sonya spends time with her family and travels to crystal-clear blue waters and sunshine.

Sonya Lamas

Colleague Experience Director

Years in HR: 13

Lamassonya@hotmail.com

DIVERSITY, INCLUSION AND THE CORPORATE MOM

BY JANINE TING JANSEN

"Experiencing racism and discrimination will not lessen, but navigating it will strengthen your resolve to influence and elevate others."

I am a passionate person who leads with integrity, truth, and a belief that I can impact, and change a mindset to be more welcoming of all individuals no matter their difference. I strive to push back on both aggressive and passive racism with the hope that I can influence others to create a better world for the person of color behind me. The physical appearance we all put forward does not tell the story of our upbringing, yet it influences our access to education, salary, and career advancement.

"Where are you from?" is a common question I receive upon meeting someone for the first time. America is such a melting pot, and I believe the curiosity behind this question overrides their self-awareness as they unconsciously probe to identify my race. Indeed, this question creates a level of discomfort that I live with every time I hear it.

I believe I encounter direct and indirect racism on a daily basis both personally and professionally. Meanwhile, I try to live my life with an innate sense of fairness that directly rubs against the systemic racism I observe and simultaneously attempt to address. My experience with racism reflects a passionate state of being proud of who I am today, and who I want to become over time, unjudged for my gender or the color of my skin.

On a personal level, I have never appreciated when people asked for my country of origin, however it has only been in the past few years that society has identified this query as a "racial microaggression." I am an American with roots that trace back to both Mexico and China. I am the child of blue-collar workers who were raised in New York City, and an observer and product of an imperfect educational system.

COMPLEXITIES AND OPPORTUNITIES

I recognize racial microaggressions when a well-intentioned individual asks someone a question about their race in an attempt to put them into a racial category. If pressed, they would admit that they would not ask that question of everyone, just people who look "different."

Having a mixed background has elicited all kinds of responses ranging from racial slurs to sexist comments, backhanded compliments praising my articulation and inquiries on the best ethnic food. Navigating the complexity of race throughout my life has led me to be a compassionate HR leader, listening to the intent of an individual and navigating whether there is truly a bias. I enjoy finding a solution in a world of gray and trying to ensure a fairer outcome. I bring a very strong point of view to the table when it comes to women, people of color, and marginalized individuals, yet enjoy working in corporate America, where I often have to navigate being a woman, a person of color, and a marginalized individual.

The challenge for diverse individuals is indeed real. I often find myself being a mediator for two different points of view while downplaying my own personal reaction. I believe my unique experience brings empathy, the business point of view, and the ability to coach against racism.

In all my educational experiences, I have felt like an outlier because of my skin color, my background, and my inability to fit into a box. When applying for college, the boxes to check for race - Hispanic (Y/N) and Asian (Y/N) and the other vague boxes that attempt to categorize applicants constantly drive home the fact that I am indeed different.

As an HR Leader who influences diversity strategy, I am often asked to draw together a story with data, analyze the workforce, and advise on how to improve our diversity representation. But I also bring my personal experience to these data-driven problems. I pride myself on being a leader who promotes a diverse culture of inclusion and acceptance for all backgrounds, while shifting a culture that eliminates racism completely. The data remains important, but it is not the full story. How does one account for the nuances of multiculturalism, gender diversity, and upbringing? For these reasons I share my story here so I may have the ability to influence change.

WORKING MOM

After college, I enrolled at The New School for a master's degree while I worked full time at a law firm in midtown Manhattan. I enjoyed conversations in the classroom on economics and racial disparities while I supported campus recruiting and diversity efforts in my first corporate role. During this time, I built upon my relationships from the Congressional Hispanic Caucus Institute (CHCI) and was one of the founders for the NY Alumni Chapter for CHCI. We built a strategy to support Latinx youth seeking educational and career opportunities.

CHCI turned me into a leader, allowed me to work for Congressman Serrano (D-NY) and surrounded me with thirty other interns who advanced my cultural learning on what it meant to be different. My time with them was fundamental in understanding the stories of my peers, how I can give back, and how to advocate for the Latinx community.

Becoming a mother was difficult and one of the most stressful yet rewarding moments of my life. The effort surpassed late nights in the office and all-nighters studying. My first hurdle was when I experienced a miscarriage on the second week of starting a new job. My husband and I had been trying, naïvely thinking things would happen on our schedule, but we found it was not as simple as choosing a date for your wedding. This loss hit me hard, emotionally. Socially, it fell into the bucket of "private," and not to be discussed openly.

Miscarriage carries a stigmatic shadow in my family and encourages inevitable questions about what I could have done to prevent it. The reality is that miscarriages happen frequently, and this would not be my last. I had my first child a year later, followed by another miscarriage two years later, and instead of starting a new job, I was let go from a job during that difficult time.

These unfortunate events led me to feel insecure, stressed, and unworthy of my career. We do not allow women to truly grieve, to take a break, and support them emotionally through their trauma. I was told to "lean-out" of my career and take it easy, which was said with good intent, but was not acceptable advice to me. My career went up and down with these events and correlated with pressure to do more, impress everyone, and find a way to "lean-in."

As any recent parent can tell you, the sleepless nights leave you a shadow of your former self. In my case, I became a full-time everything - nursing mom/wife/employee who squeezed in nursing by pumping in a closet-like room, navigating meetings throughout the day, hustling meals, and responding to the endless needs of my young children.

What was my struggle as a young mom navigating corporate America? I had to navigate multiple sources of child support between daycare, babysitters and my parents, who worked full time but helped me when they could. My husband worked twenty-four- hour shifts so we made the decision to enroll our children in full-time day care. I was commuting more than an hour each way to work, pumping two or three times a day to feed my baby, and trying to network and take in every career-changing meeting because it was the right thing to do. This left me in a quandary, wondering how to maximize the precious time I had. The answer I found varied depending on the day and I found very few people who empathized with me.

Often, I will be in a conversation with men who compare my experiences with those of their wives or daughters concerning education, motherhood, or the workplace. In doing so, they tend to marginalize the woman who is overcoming systemic racism and gender bias. The comments range from "my wife was up all night with our child" or "she struggles at drop-off as well" and the empathy feels lacking because they are not associating their own personal journey. These well-intended comments highlight the gap that exists for women. I have intimately felt the burden of feeling the separation from my child, the despair at drop-off, commuting to the office, sacrificing a lunch hour for "pumping" as a nursing mother, and rushing to pick up my child at the end of the day. There is a very real challenge in coordinating these activities, the emotions of being a mother of young children, and remaining present in your career. When men talk about how their wives or partners handle being a mother, they infer that they do not intimately experience being a parent. Someone else is doing the emotional, physical job of caring for their children.

My ambition to have it all often pushed me to the limit. I had finally earned my seat at the table, my right to my title, and I refused to give up. My children are still young as I write this today, and I continue to feel conflicted with the priority of the day or week, but do accept the confidence that has resulted from my simultaneous push to achieve and foster their flourishing lives that wait for no one.

I have frequently found myself working with a

group of individuals who were vastly different from me in gender, race, and socioeconomic background. As a young mother in a career role, I am often asked to speak on my experiences while also navigating my feelings of inadequacy. I believe sharing differences is important. It creates a context where difference is influential to shape a culture of acceptance and brings to light the present barriers for women and people of color.

However, being on display always came with risk. Psychologically, the "imposter syndrome" I have experienced in each phase of my life as college applicant, college graduate, HR professional, and a working mother often creeps in to undermine what you bring to the table. It is difficult to acknowledge that your education, experience, and innate willingness to achieve greater results can be undermined by just one racist comment. One thoughtless remark can make you second-guess your credentials and reintroduce a need to work even harder to prove yourself – a vicious cycle that is not sustainable and is destructive in nature. By discussing imposter syndrome with trusted peers and networks, I can address this social construct and directly do something to shore up my confidence and support others.

ADVICE FROM THE FUTURE

If I could advise my younger self, I would encourage

her to live life to the fullest, enjoy every experience and consider every "no" an opportunity to find a "yes." The stress of that paycheck will ease over time and you will have the freedom to choose the role that fits best. Experiencing racism and discrimination will not lessen but navigating it will strengthen your resolve to influence and elevate others. Building a family will be one of the most challenging opportunities you take on and fuel you emotionally to do more professionally.

You will develop strategies to mitigate racism and its impact on your psyche. You will find teachable moments to drive change and reduce the stigma that surrounds women and people of color. Your ability to bridge the gap with those of good intent, and those who display racist actions – even when they are the same person - will be highly valued at any table you join. Continue to fight racism, gender bias, and enjoy being a mother; the struggle is real, and nothing is ever easy, but there are great rewards for continuing to drive change with your passion for doing the right thing. As a mother, there is a new generation looking to you as a model, and a new generation to lead in new directions.

REFLECT AND RISE

As a mentor, leader, and passionate HR lead, I frequently meet with youth to discuss their college aspirations, career interests, and their growth in an entry-level role. Access to a college education is a barrier for most communities of color and something I have experienced first-hand. Here are some things that young, aspiring HR professionals should remember:

- **The key to succeeding in education is to persist, prioritize, and advocate for yourself.** Turn every denial, rejection and no, into a yes by learning from it.

- **When you accept your first job offer seek guidance from your peers, mentor, and sponsors that believe in you.** Choose to control your life-changing moments by learning and growing.

- **For young parents, choose the moments to be with your children but also prepare for when you will miss a moment.** Your children will remember the ones they want and forget the others – the key is listening to their priorities too.

As I shared my journey of navigating the corporate corridor as a woman of color, I would encourage you to be proud of your uniqueness and demonstrate empathy for others who are singled-out. Allyship comes in all forms and we can lead by educating others, rather than being reactionary to racism. Find your strength at the table and lean-in with integrity, confidence, and pride.

BIOGRAPHY

Janine is a third-generation American of Mexican and Chinese descent. Her maternal and paternal grandparents immigrated to the U.S. from China and Mexico, with stops in California, Texas, Louisiana, and finally New York City. They married in NYC and had multiple children, including her parents, who were raised next door to each other on the lower east side of Manhattan. Life in multicultural New York City influenced the way she was raised.

Janine's grandparents supported their families by serving in the U.S. Navy, sewing in sweatshops, waiting tables in Chinese restaurants, and managing a charitable association (a gathering place for recent immigrants), in Chinatown. Her father was a NYC firefighter during 9/11, and her mother raised Janine and two siblings before navigating a career at Walmart. Janine was the first college graduate in her family, and her world view is influenced by a hard-working family who loves without restraint and is often mistaken for various races, but never the right ones. She views her journey through corporate America as opportunistic and is drawn to it by her innate fairness and work ethic. Friends of Janine describe her as determined to succeed and assist others with their personal and professional journeys.

Janine Ting Jansen

Director, People Partner

Years in HR: 14

jtingjansen@gmail.com

LinkedIn.com/in/jtingjansen

WORKING HARD TO NEVER GIVE UP

BY GRISELDA RODRIGUEZ

"Always look for ways to improve yourself."

I grew up in Little Village, a community in the south Lawndale area of Chicago, Illinois, known for its Mexican population. It is a picturesque town. Visitors are welcomed by a large arch with a clock in the center, as you would see in Mexico, that says *Bienvenidos to Little Village*, or "Welcome to Little Village." I loved growing up there. I didn't feel judged for how I communicated, my appearance, or where I came from. I belonged.

KEEP BUSY, DON'T STOP

I did well in school and once I had a job and a car, I felt invincible and did whatever I wanted. I became rebellious and hard to control. During one of my arguments with my mom, I decided to move out. That's when my life changed.

I was only 16 years old and for a while I was on my

own. Soon after, I decided that I was ready to move in with my boyfriend. We got an apartment, got married, and had a child. My life went from being a strong, independent young woman with a lot of dreams, to a stay-at-home mom and having a hard time keeping my marriage intact. With time, we grew apart and went in different directions, and suddenly, I was a 24-year-old single mom.

Being a young single mom was not going to be easy, but I couldn't give up. One thing I learned from my mom was resiliency. In the toughest of times is when she fought the hardest. She is the strongest person I know, and if she could be tough, I could be tough.

While I was married, I worked on earning my associate degree but wanted to do more to provide for my son and I. I decided to go back to school and earn my bachelor's degree. When I told people my plans, they were not as supportive as I hoped. They would say things such as "what you have accomplished so far is good enough" or, "why do you want to make things harder on yourself? You are setting yourself up for failure." I knew they were looking out for my best interest, but my gut told me it was something I had to do. I was determined.

I enrolled in school and told my loved ones my decision. There was no changing my mind, and I would need their support to succeed. I was working full time, going to school full time, and parenting as a single mom. It was hard and I would not have accomplished this without the help of my mother who was there for me and helped me with my son.

Sometimes it felt like I was being selfish, giving up my time with my son to go to school. I would ask myself, "What kind of mother am I? I should focus on parenting, not school. Am I a good mother? Will my son remember this time in his life when mom was in school and not with him?"

These were all hard questions that I didn't have the answers to. I tend to be an introvert and I didn't have many friends to confide in and ask if I was making the right choices. I knew, deep in my heart, that I needed to see this through. I told myself I was making the right decision. If my son ever resented me, I would be able to explain my choices. I knew he would resent me much more for failing to do the best I could to provide him with a better life and set a good example.

My life became a blur. The time with my son was limited. Soon I realized that spending quality time with him was going to get me through the hard times. I woke up at five o'clock every morning, got ready for work, and dropped my son off at my mom's house. I took the "L" train to get to my eight-to-five job, took the train to go to school from six to nine-thirty at night and then took the "L" back home.

Usually my son was already asleep by the time I got home. Sometimes he would sleep over at grandma's house, so I didn't have to wake him up. At times I would pick him up, even if he was asleep, just to see him. Once I got settled at home I would be up until midnight or later, working on homework. I would go to bed and start the routine all over again the next day.

I don't remember being exhausted, although thinking about it now makes me feel tired. I only remember being energized. I had something I needed to accomplish, and there was no time to be exhausted. I needed to push through. Maybe I just kept going so I didn't have time to think about all the things that worried me. Keep busy, don't think. Keep busy, don't stop.

Before I went back to school, I had a couple of jobs in staffing and recruiting. This made me develop a love/hate relationship with the industry. I really enjoyed meeting new people, helping them find employment, and working in different industries. I have tons of respect for people who work in recruiting; it is hard work and they often get mistreated. They are hustlers and they roll up their sleeves to get the job done and don't leave until it is.

Staffing and recruiting gave me a crash course into the world of human resources (HR). Then, just a few months before completing my degree, I was laid off. I had very little savings. They got me through a couple of months of rent and bills while I focused on my final paper and finishing school.

When I graduated, I immediately started interviewing. I reached out to some agencies to help me find a job. I was fortunate enough to get several offers, including my first official role as an HR specialist in the corporate world. With no way of getting to work, I took my offer letter to a car dealership so I could get a used, dependable car. The old one repeatedly broke down on the way to several interviews and was beyond repair. This job was my lifeline. I needed to take care of my son and I. This was how I was going to do it.

My parents were proud of me. Having a stable job, my own apartment, and a dependable car was a huge accomplishment. I knew this was just the beginning of my journey. I had a lot more to give and was going to work hard to prove that I deserved the job I had.

THE CORPORATE WORLD

My new position provided HR assistance to a warehouse facility that had over three hundred employees, the majority of them Hispanic or Latino. I onboarded new hires, counseled, coached, trained, and processed terminations. The warehouse distributed food to stores throughout the Midwest, including familiar brands like Ariel, Goya, and La Preferida; these products are called "specialty items."

I felt at home in the large Hispanic population there. My favorite part of the job was doing town halls or large meetings. It was my opportunity to put my translation skills to the test and impress upper management. They were always complimentary about how well I could quickly translate in a live meeting. I wasn't perfect, but I took it as a challenge to do better next time.

This job had its ups and downs. The hardest part of my job was letting employees go. Whether it was for due cause or a layoff, it was never easy. Every single person has a reason to work, take care of their family, provide a roof over their head, pay bills, and put food on the table. When you take away their ability to provide, it's hard.

One piece of advice I'd like to share with other HR professionals is that when you are going to release someone, do it with respect, empathy, and care. Regardless of what a person does to lose their job they deserve to be treated with dignity.

Working in a warehouse environment helped me feel comfortable but other things about my job were not. The employees in the warehouse reminded me of family members or neighbors. They were easy to talk to and relate to. My peers and upper management seemed different from me. There was not a lot of diversity in the corporate setting and it made me wonder if I could grow there.

To gain credibility, I had to work twice as hard. Often, I was the only female in a room. It felt intimidating. I would motivate myself by thinking, *Hey, they hired me.* They have to see something good in me.

I also had a great mentor, who happened to be my boss. He was encouraging, supportive, and has been one of the best teachers in my life. Sometimes I wondered how someone so unlike me wanted to help me. He gave me lots of advice and tough love, always with my best interest at heart. The head of HR was also inspirational to me. She was the first female leader I ever met. I admired her for being strong, hardworking, and kind. She genuinely cared about the people around her. Both of them were influential in my career and were always in my corner.

NEW GOALS

As I matured in my career and grew complacent, I set goals to grow and push myself harder. I felt that in my current role, there was not much left to learn. I wondered what else could I do? Or where should I go from here. My vision was larger; I wanted to eventually lead an entire HR team. How could I accomplish this? I thought hard about it and met with one of my mentors. I wanted to ask her for advice. I needed help to figure out how to do it.

I was lucky enough to have the opportunity to lead the benefits team, but I was worried I couldn't do it. I honestly didn't know much about benefits, other than the high-level information I explained during new hire orientation.

I decided to take a leap. I left my boss to spread my wings and learn the complexity of managing benefit plans. To say the least, it was hard. There was a lot to figure out and I was scared, but I persisted. Failing wasn't an option.

I have learned so much and continue to grow. Now, my role consists of project management, overseeing health and welfare and retirement plans for more than six thousand employees across the U.S. But the best part is mentoring my team.

I'm in a place in my career where I can pay it forward--sharing my failures, experiences, and my successes with those who look up to me for guidance. I hope that one day some young girl or boy from Little Village, struggling to find their place, can read my story and say if a Mexican single mom was able to push through and accomplish what she wanted, I can too.

REFLECT AND RISE

Growing your career will come with a lot of struggles. Surround yourself with good people, and if you are lucky, you will find a few good mentors. Listen to the advice people give you, some of it will be great, but some of it will not suit you and those you can disregard. Be resilient. Being the hardest worker in the room will pay off. And always remember…

- You belong, and if you don't believe it, fake it until it becomes true.

- You are loved. There is someone out there who knows how special and worthy you are.

- Help others. When you have paved the path for yourself, reach back and pull someone up with you because we all need a little help.

- Fight for what is right, and when the time comes to deliver bad news, be kind, gentle, and allow people to keep their humanity. And finally, ...

- Be a learner. Always look for ways to improve yourself.

BIOGRAPHY

Griselda Rodriguez, PHR Certified since 2014, is a graduate of Robert Morris University, now known as Roosevelt University. She has a bachelor's degree in business administration with a concentration in management and seventeen years of progressive HR experience. She currently works for KeHE Distributors, LLC as Director of Benefits, where she oversees the health, retirement and wellness plans for more than six thousand employees nationwide. She also is part of KeHE's Diversity and Inclusion Council whose mission is to improve employee engagement by reducing systemic processes that support unconscious bias and establish awareness of D&I throughout the company and industry.

Griselda is engaged to Juan, the love of her life, and has two wonderful children, Alan and Haley, who are the center of her world. She enjoys weekly bootcamp sessions, running, and has a newfound respect for yoga. Before the pandemic, Griselda enjoyed traveling for pleasure and traveling on service trips with her current employer. Griselda is an eternal learner and believes in self-improving by reading a good book, listening to a new podcast, or attending an interesting training session. Her favorite recent reads are Becoming by Michele Obama and Between the World and Me, by Ta-Nehisi Coates.

Griselda Rodriguez, PHR

Benefits Director

Years in HR: 17

griselda_rgz@yahoo.com

Linkedin.com/in/griselda-rodriguez-phr-9381b27

FROM SURIVING TO THRIVING

BY STEPHANIE MARTINEZ

"The path to success is never easy, so take time to acknowledge all you've accomplished."

My name is Stephanie Martinez and I grew up on the southside of Chicago and was the youngest of four children from a loving, crazy family. My parents made education a critical focus of our lives. We also valued faith, hard work, perseverance, being respectful, setting high expectations, and the freedom to pursue our interests. My mother gave us the gift of empathy, compassion, and faith. My father instilled us with strength, and taught us to reach for that higher ground, and about the world of organizing and business. I felt safe, protected by funny storytellers (like my sister, Lisa, and my brother, Jonathan), surrounded by love, great cooks, and big family parties. It was my safe foundation which helped me surpass the challenges in my life.

One of those challenges was surviving a physically

and verbally abusive relationship in my high school and college years. My daughter, Michelle, was a great gift, but I endured post-traumatic stress and shame from that relationship. I knew that God had called me to do something greater with my life and my daughter deserved more from me than I could initially give her.

UP THE LADDER

Like a phoenix rising from the ashes, I would rise too. I had to see myself as a survivor, not a victim. With my family's help, I created a plan for our future, beginning with getting an education. I went to school full time in the evenings and worked as a bank teller during the day until I received my bachelor's degree in industrial/organizational psychology. That was my first win! My daughter saw me graduate from college, which made my heart soar.

From there, I kept building my knowledge and received my Society of Human Resource Management Certified Professional (SHRM-CP) and Professional in Human Resources (PHR) certifications. I read books, listened to podcasts, and got my Association for Talent Development (ATD) Training certificate. Most importantly of all, I kept learning. I listened to what was said and unsaid in work meetings, attempting to decode the power plays, the strategy that went into the messaging, and the relational dynamics. I absorbed it all to become a more valuable employee.

It wasn't easy to be a single, working parent. I had no work/life balance and was determined to have it all. I wanted to be a strong/independent female role model for my daughter. I can't say I did it perfectly, but I managed to do the best I could. I gave my daughter a safe, loving home, put meals on the table, helped her with school and extracurricular activities, and paid all my bills. I lived paycheck to paycheck for a long time, but I knew my hard work and perseverance would pay off if I remained vigilant about my goals and achieving them.

My career path was all about building my toolbox. Although I know what my passion is now that I'm in my forties, it was a culmination of high and low experiences that led me to my true calling to be a consultant. I knew I loved solving problems and having lots of variety in my job because I love a good challenge. I also wanted to make a difference in people's lives. I was determined to build the ideal background for a consultant role to accept when the time was right.

I knew that consultants worked across a wide variety of industries, understood different organizational structures and dynamics, thought strategically, identified gaps and solved problems quickly, communicated and led projects well, and were self-motivated. I took my time working for all different types of companies as an internal HR generalist/business partner in the following industries:

education, hospital, financial services, manufacturing, and an employee benefit brokerage firm. I also learned about my strengths and areas of opportunity with DISC assessments and coaching from my mentors. When I finally had the opportunity to run an HR consulting practice, I had built the leadership skills to advise my clients in the C-suite. Next, I learned how to devise effective strategies, build client relationships, and expand my network.

THE MARVEL OF MENTORS

My mentors truly changed my world. I had heard about mentorship, but always felt awkward asking someone to be mine. Instead, my mentor relationships developed organically from my managers, my colleagues, and key people in my network. They are so numerous that it would take this whole book to cover them, so I'll just mention my top seven. These mentors inspired me to reach for something bigger than myself; they all had qualities or skills I didn't have, but wanted; and we all shared common values.

They include Michelle McGovern, vice president of Mesirow Financial when I was an HR generalist; Mark Matuscak, CEO at Benefitdecisions when I was leading up the HR consulting practice; Olga Camargo, the senior vice president in the investment advisory group at Mesirow Financial, when I was an HR generalist; Maricela Garcia,

CEO of Gads Hill Center, who selected me for their board; Dave McKeon, the managing director of the HR consulting practice at Executive Coaching Connections who inspired me to start my own business; Carol Semrad, Principal of C. Semrad & Associates and treasurer for Chicago SHRM, who helped me obtain new clients and encouraged me to join the Chicago SHRM Education Committee (which I love); Bob Mallo, who is the president of Corporate Connection Consultants, and helped me land my first client when I started my HR consulting business; and last, but not least, my father, Peter Martinez, who coached me while establishing my business. These mentors came along at different times in my life when I needed to learn a new skill or overcome a challenge in my career.

My mentors helped me find my voice and add value in the moment. I'm a terribly quiet person, and I like to ponder and analyze things before I speak, which some leaders perceived as lack of interest or confidence. Being a female Latina HR person puts everything you do, say, and wear on display. I think at times I wanted to blend in but blending in doesn't get you anywhere.

My mentors also taught me how to read the room and communicate with all types of people. This comes from recognizing people's DISC styles and getting to know your leaders well enough to understand their self-interests.

I always respected my mentor's time. I had to do

my part to maintain the mentor/mentee relationship which meant initiating and scheduling our meetings, implementing their advice, following through with suggestions, and always coming prepared to our meetings with an agenda. Even today, I continue to maintain touch points with my mentors to build upon our relationship.

THE CHALLENGE OF THE MULTICULTURAL

All my life I have struggled to embrace my own ethnicity and multicultural background. My grandparents were immigrants from El Salvador, Germany, Czechoslovakia (now Czech Republic), and Poland. In the 1930's, when my parents were growing up, it was better to blend in than speak your natural born language. I grew up in an English-speaking household, raised on American traditions. When I was tapped by Olga Camargo and Maricela Garcia to get involved in various diversity initiatives, I felt like an imposter. Who was I to speak about the Latino community when I knew nothing about it? Both of those women taught me that although my heritage was different, my passion, knowledge, and desire to make an impact was all I needed. I embraced their faith in me and took a leadership role on the board of the nonprofit organization, Gads Hill Center. I also started the young professionals board. Both of these experiences enhanced my network, built my leadership skills, and helped me understand what it takes to run a nonprofit business.

If you're a giver, then you want more. I felt a strong desire to help others, similar to what my mentors had done for me. I invested my time in causes that aligned with my values (family, faith, education, youth, mentorship), especially giving back to the Latino community and at-risk youth at Gads Hill Center. I also was the program coordinator for the Northwestern Youth Impact Program. Each of these programs connected with my own success story and offered kids the opportunity to build up their confidence and participate in STEM programs. We aligned them with teachers and mentors they admired, and they had a safe place to learn and be themselves. I am overjoyed to know that we played a small part in helping these kids "dream a bigger dream."

The opportunity to give back doesn't end there. Now that I've been running my own HR consulting company for the last two years, I see that I have the unique opportunity to uplift entrepreneurs and other women. If I can give advice and share what I've learned with others so they don't have to experience what I did, then I'm happy to do so.

The last, but not least challenge I had to conquer was building my network. Being a quiet/introverted person, I'm a big fan of one-on-one conversations, but ask me to go into a large room full of people I don't know, and I'll run the other direction. Three of my mentors were serial Networkers—Michelle, Olga, and Mark. They sent me to Crain's Networking Events, HRMAC (Human Resources Management Association of Chicago) and SHRM events, had me write articles for a magazine, provide training for the Entrepreneurs Organization (EO) and finally, take on some speaking engagements. It was tough facing my fear in the beginning, but soon I began enjoying meetings and learning new things about these strangers. Before I knew it, I had built up a great network I call my "board of directors."

Whether you work in internal or external HR, you need to know people who specialize in things that you don't. You will find that these are the people you go to for advice, share referrals/resources, and even recommend you for future job opportunities. Your network is also there to keep you sharp and bring new ideas and trends to your attention. The "Go Giver" gives more, so always return the favor. Keep your contacts in mind when there's a business opportunity that would benefit them. We are all in this together.

My experiences in HR have taught me to be a strong independent woman who may have been the underdog but is very capable of rising to the challenge. I needed to fight to achieve more for me and my daughter. I set goals and wouldn't let the setbacks get me down; I continued driving forward. I would not be a victim and changed the narrative, so I had control of my own story and how it ends. Being the underdog can be fun, because when you bring your "A" game, people can't refute your right to be there. So, go the extra mile! Regardless of what position we hold, we have the opportunity to be a leader. Be the kind of leader you'd want to follow.

In closing, I get my strength from my family and my faith. I love being at church and surrounding myself in the word of God. My family keeps me grounded and provides support when I need it. I also had to learn self-care because you need to be mindful of your limitations and how valuable a break can be. I love nature, going for long walks, exercising, taking vacations, and spending time laughing with my family and friends.

The path to success is never easy, so take time to acknowledge all you've accomplished. Give yourself some grace. I love what Michelle Obama said in her documentary, Becoming: "When they go low, we go high." The world of business can be tough, so be professional and choose your words wisely. As in this presidential race, people will remember what you said **AND** how you made them feel. Above all else, keep reaching for more. If the sky's the limit, what's next for you?

REFLECT AND RISE

My final thoughts to anyone going into HR:

- **Do your homework.** Talk to experts in HR so you can discover what gets you excited about the field and what credentials you need to succeed in your desired role. Research your ideal companies and the experience they look for in their applicants.

- **Network like crazy and start to build your board of directors.** I have built my network up with individuals I know/like/and trust as well as those who have expertise in various areas. Your network will make you more valuable than you could ever imagine.

- **Do what it takes to earn your place at the table. Nothing comes easy.** You have to show people that you can handle all different types of scenarios before they'll give you the keys to the castle.

- **Take charge of your career by learning as much as you can from books, people, online learning, experiences, etc.** I missed great learning opportunities in my career because I didn't think I could add one more thing to my plate, and it was a huge mistake. Try to say yes to as many things that you can, because you never know what opportunity may arise.

- **Take time to celebrate your successes and how you've grown**. Thank those that have helped you get there.

- **Give more than you receive.** Read the book, The Go-Giver, by Bob Burg and John David Mann. I always make time to mentor people starting their own business or advancing in their HR career.

BIOGRAPHY

Stephanie Martinez is a successful HR leader, consultant, facilitator and coach with twenty years of experience in HR, working with small to mid-sized organizations to customize solutions around their people issues. She focuses on four key areas: talent solutions, developing and retaining talent, getting the organization in compliance, and establishing a strong foundation and structure for HR that aligns with the business. Stephanie is also a results-driven leader with extensive experience, strategic planning, organizational effectiveness, executive coaching, and employee relations as a HR practitioner and consultant.

Stephanie enjoys working with stakeholders, senior executives, HR leaders, and first line managers on the people issues that are prohibiting their organization from reaching their full potential. She has worked with organizations on setting their direction through SWOT analysis/strategic planning sessions; creating training sessions around constructive conversations and managing performance; and defining a talent acquisition strategy which attracts talent and enhances the culture and productivity of the organization. Stephanie strives to work with her clients as a trusted partner and sincerely cares about making a difference in their organization. It's not about her, it's about them.

Stephanie was born and raised on the south side of Chicago and has a 23-year-old daughter, Michelle.

Stephanie Martinez, SHRM-CP, PHR

CEO & Founder, HRDesigned4U, LLC

Years in HR: 20

smartinez@hrdesigned4u.com

Linkedin.com/in/stephanie-martinez-1018/

FAITH, PERSEVERANCE, AND RESILIENCE

BY EDITH PACHECO

"We all have the ability to become who we are meant to be with faith, perseverance, and resilience."

It was the winter of 1997, in Rosemont, Illinois when I walked into the human resources office to apply for a job at the Hyatt hotel where my dad worked. I was eighteen years old. My employer had gone bankrupt, and my papa knew about an opening in the accounting department. I had only stayed at a hotel twice in my life and didn't know anything about the hotel business. My dad believed in me, even though things in my life up to that point, had been very difficult for my family.

FROM TEEN TO ADULT

In the Fall of 1994, at the age of sixteen, I learned I was pregnant. The one thing my parents were afraid of and had warned me about continuously had happened. I was not

225

supposed to be another pregnant teen; I was supposed to go to college. They were shattered. I did the right and honorable thing for my family and moved in with my boyfriend, which was the expectation in the Mexican culture. Pregnancy out of wedlock means the man should marry the woman and take responsibility for her and their child. It also meant that I was to immediately assume the duties of both wife and mother as a teenager.

This is when my life changed forever. Within twenty-four hours, I left my childhood behind and moved into his house. Nothing could have prepared me for the reality of the sad, broken home I moved into. There were days that mother and son would not speak to each other. There was a history of domestic violence and verbal abuse. I felt like I was in a Cinderella story but with no happy ending in sight. Resilience became my key to survival.

I gave birth to a precious, tiny, baby boy the summer of 1995. His name is Josue but he prefers to be called Josh these days. Josue became my strength and my reason to always strive for more. I started my senior year of high school that Fall. It was very challenging to take care of a home, a child, and attend school. However, despite the difficulty, I graduated on time, on stage with my class.

As I look back, I realize how blessed I am that God put so many people in my life to help guide me. One of them was an academic counselor, Luis. He helped me and many of my friends navigate high school. He was the adult advocate we needed. He knew my home situation and that I was looking for a job, and not to attend college. He connected me with a colleague who helped single mothers get out of the welfare system. She worked with me to get an internship at an office which provided on-the-job training. After a couple of months, the internship turned into a job. As I write this, it's amazing to realize I received exactly what I needed at the time.

On the job, I learned office etiquette, how to use a computer, and everything I needed to know to run an office. I was able to create a resume to help me find another office job, especially after the company announced they were going bankrupt. And this brings me back to the day I applied at the Hyatt Regency O'Hare.

REACHING HEIGHTS AT HYATT

I met with the employment manager who talked through some job openings, including the accounting role and an administrative assistant role in the human resources department. Halfway through the interview, he asked me if I would be interested in the HR role because it was a good fit with my experience. Being fluent in Spanish was also to my advantage. Days later, I received three calls with three job offers, including my first-choice position at a hospital. As much as I wanted to take the hospital job, I wanted to work where my dad worked. I accepted the administrative assistant role with Hyatt. I can honestly say that if I had to choose again, I would have made the same choice.

I was the only person of color in the office at my new position. It was a culture shock coming from a predominately Hispanic high school and community. In the beginning, I struggled with having the right professional wardrobe and fitting in. I really didn't have anything in common with the people in the office. At times I felt ashamed for not having the college experience my Caucasian colleagues did. However, despite the various obstacles, I wanted to do well and could not disappoint my dad. It was a big responsibility for a girl who had minimal work experience and no HR background. I had to learn about the role that human resources played at the company. I think that turning on my switch to adulthood as a teen allowed me to step into this role with determination and maturity.

As a novice administrative assistant in HR, the first thing I learned about was employee relations. I was introduced to employees of all departments. When the word got out that I spoke Spanish, I was in business! I learned that our office was there to support all employees of the hotel. I didn't know this then but being able to serve others is what motivates me. The challenges I faced personally allowed me to care and empathize for the matters that were brought to us, from helping someone to fill out a vacation form, to listening about a problem, to answering questions about benefits.

I was taught to screen applicants for open positions for different functions. I got to know the hiring managers and learned more about the hotel business. I met many people from all different backgrounds who were seeking employment. I was able to help guide those who were eager for a job in hospitality but didn't know what they could do. It reminded me of how I started in my role, and how I now had the opportunity to pay it forward. I learned the importance of building relationships, trust, and credibility. The humility my mom and dad taught me was instrumental in working with people from all walks of life. It also helped tremendously that my dad had so many great relationships with the hotel staff and they were open to come to me for help.

My career in HR really kicked into gear after my first-year anniversary. There were trials and tribulations during that first year that made me doubt if I would make it, but we all have the ability to become who we are meant to be with faith, perseverance, and resilience. My director and I didn't understand each other, and I felt like I was always walking on eggshells until she transferred to another location. The new director, Sharon Edbrooke (RIP), came and within one month of seeing my work, nominated me for the employee of the month award. She saw my potential and believed in me. She listened to the feedback of the managers in the office who vouched for my work ethic. She changed the course of my career and helped me flourish and grow in so many ways, both professionally and personally. Her leadership style was admirable and inspirational. She promoted me to a coordinator role that increased the scope of my responsibilities. I learned about benefits for union and non-union plans, as well as how to handle and lead the investigation for workers' compensation cases.

My next promotion was to a management role, prompted by the director of accounting, Gabe Castrillon. He approached me to take a management role doing payroll, but instead I pursued a manager role in my own department that became available. I talked to Sharon and put my name in the hat for the role that became my next position, employment manager. It was a proud moment and a great accomplishment for me. My experience at Hyatt Regency O'Hare would be the education I needed to launch the rest of my career in human resources.

A CHANGE OF SCENE

In 2002, I became the manager of benefits and employment at the Hyatt Lodge in Oak Brook, Illinois. I was comfortable with many of the duties in this role and I thought it would be easy to transition. I was wrong. Even though the hotel was much smaller with fewer employees, the HR office was also smaller. I really missed my friends and my routine at O'Hare. I was the new kid on the block and had to earn trust and build relationships with all the staff. I didn't appreciate this then, but now I know that new challenges and getting out of my comfort zone is always when growth happens. I learned to be more inquisitive and analytical.

Word got out that the company was hiring a third-party vendor to administer benefits. I worried that there would be reduction in the workforce for my role across the company. This had me looking at my next role after three years. My manager at the time approached me about a human resources information systems (HRIS) coordinator role at the corporate office. I struggled a bit with accepting it because it was not a manager role and I knew nothing about systems, outside of being an end user. However, I could not see myself leaving Hyatt if there was going to be downsizing.

I applied and interviewed with the hiring manager, Jeanne Kalinowski (RIP). She was implementing a new HR Information system for more than one hundred U.S. hotels. I had no idea what it meant to work in an HRIS role and thought for sure I was not qualified for the job. However, Jeanne saw something special in a young woman who was eager to work and open to learning; a person who knew the hospitality business, the culture, and brought the field perspective of an end user.

Jeanne's leadership style was impressive. She was brilliant and her intelligence was at times intimidating, yet her smile and laughter were warm and contagious. She taught me another side of human resources that I hated and loved at the same time. I had learned to be an HR person, yet somehow with her guidance and training, I became an avid systems person. She assigned me to audit data, a skill I didn't know I had. I analyzed and caught uncaptured discrepancies. She taught me how to fine tune our processes, address the discrepancies found, and create process flows. It was uncomfortable at times and I didn't think I could further my career in HRIS. I hesitated to take on a more technical role that would advance my career.

Instead, I decided to pursue my college degree. I told Jeanne and she supported my decision and offered me project work to do remotely during the three years I was in school. On summer or winter breaks, I would work onsite. This was very strategic on her end as I was able to stay current with our function and have visibility with other departments. I graduated with a teaching degree but decided not to pursue teaching.

Instead, I took a corporate human resources specialist role to regain my full-time status with the company. Eventually, I began my climb again, first to a retirement benefits analyst, then to senior analyst, and finally, to my current role as benefits manager. In this role, I continue to have the opportunity to impact and teach others.

Today, I lead a significant function in the company with a small, but mighty team. I take what I have learned from current and past leaders and apply it to the work I do. I especially lead with the style of my previous mentors, Sharon and Jeanne (RIP). They taught me that a daring leader is not afraid to be wrong and to be vulnerable. To not see color or circumstances but only the potential that each of us has to make an impact.

REFLECT AND RISE

With faith, perseverance, and resilience, we can become who we are meant to be. How do we do that?

- Build genuine relationships and don't be afraid to be vulnerable
- Each experience you encounter will teach you something
- Invest in your personal and professional development and growth
- Have mentors and sponsors

BIOGRAPHY

Edith Pacheco has a passion for being an agent for change. She strives to make the world a better place by demonstrating kindness and serving others. Her drive comes from her own life experiences ranging from childhood to motherhood. She uses her struggles and triumphs to share her story of faith, perseverance, resilience, and hope.

Over the years she has had substantial personal and professional growth and development. Through this work she has overcome self-doubt and is rewriting her story. These new chapters speak of her faith and how prayer has changed her life. She is learning to trust, believe, and live out her most authentic life while discovering her purpose, one day at a time.

A life-long learner, Edith received her B.A. in elementary education at Northern Illinois University. She has more than twenty years of HR and hospitality experience. This rewarding career and industry have enriched her life with many long-lasting friendships.

She was born and raised in Chicago and is first generation Mexican American, the oldest of four, and a proud mom to her son, Josue. She embraces her roots and loves to learn more about her heritage through travel.

Edith Pacheco

Benefits Manager

Years in HR: 23

epacheco78@gmail.com

Linkedin.com/in/edith-pacheco-63387a11

FINDING YOUR LIGHT: A STORY OF PURPOSE AND DETERMINATION

BY ISABEL MONTES

"As we go through our journey, we should be opening doors for others".

Beneath the story I am about to tell you lies my conviction that the human resources professionals who can really make an important contribution to their companies and to society, are those whose personal purpose is aligned with the role of HR. The HR function has helped me to achieve my purpose, and that alignment has been worth all the commitment and determination in the world.

TOUGH AND TENDER

My career in human resources started by accident—I wanted to be in supply chain. I am an industrial engineer by education; I like to know and change how things work to make them more efficient. Before I graduated college,

I applied for an internship in supply chain with Procter & Gamble. I was selected.

It turned out P&G really liked my profile but not for supply chain. "After all the assessments, we believe that yours is a profile for human resources," they said. I disagreed with their assessments. I thought human resources was not for me. In my mind at the time, HR was about making people happy and holding hands. However, I felt special because I was selected among hundreds of people and I decided to believe what they saw in me. Something inside me told me it was the right move.

When I was twenty-one years old, I moved to Bogotá, hours from my beloved city of Cali, Colombia. My position was in a hair care factory, an environment I really like. I got the chance to see what HR really is: a function that participates in the creation of the company strategy and enables it. I immediately fell in love. I saw the systematic thinking and process-oriented functions, and which ones could be improved to be more efficient, all while touching people's lives.

With P&G I faced the unfortunate reality of having to shut down the factory. As part of my first work experience, I had to support the layoffs of three hundred people. I saw three hundred families lose their main source of income, but I learned how to do it in a compassionate way. This experience confirmed that HR is a function that requires strong reasoning, compassion, and empathy. It answers the question, how can people have the best experience in the midst of whatever is happening in the business? It challenges us to create strategies in which we balance the business and the people and aim at the crux where they both win. It simultaneously requires us to be empathetic, strategic, and consider the best options for the person and the enterprise.

So suddenly, I was in the HR field. When reflecting on how the P&G's assessment turned out to be correct, I realized that in a group setting I tend to be the person who organizes the plan, asks others to contribute, and coordinates. I can be very pragmatic. I also studied music for many years, playing the saxophone. I have balanced the mindset of an engineer with a deep love for the arts. HR was the perfect match for me — rationality driven by the heart. Also, a voice inside confirmed that this was the right path for me. I listened to that voice, trusted it, and my inner wisdom has never failed me since.

A LIGHT FOR ME

Years later, life brought me to the U.S. I had limited English skills and I didn't know anyone. I was also resolute to be that Colombian who came to this country and left a mark. I wanted to eventually be the HR leader for Latin America at a U.S.-based company. Once that goal became clear, I was consistent and focused. I didn't lose sleep over it or obsess about it. I knew that sooner or later I would find the path to achieve my dream. My inner wisdom assured me of it.

I remember driving through downtown Seattle, looking at the small lights in the office buildings and thinking, *it's impossible that in all of those lights there isn't a job for me. One of those lights will be my next office.* There was simply no other option.

It was not easy. I received my authorization to work in the country just days after 9/11 happened. There were no jobs. I saw an opening as a cashier and took it. I cleaned bathrooms and offered to have the opening shift at four o'clock in the morning to add extra hours. And every chance I got, I would go back downtown, look at the lights, and assure myself that eventually, one of those lights would be for me.

During the journey of achieving my professional dream, I was focused on doing what could get me closer to it. In my case, that meant juggling at least three balls simultaneously: handling the cash register, studying for a master's program in human resources, and strategically looking for a position in HR. My last job in Colombia had been as a business consultant for Arthur Andersen, working with SAP for HR. As a newly arrived immigrant, I felt at a disadvantage competing against native English speakers. I knew that the technology skills I had would give me a better chance. I understood my value, found my niche, and as soon as I saw an opportunity, I jumped at it. I found a job that was going to take me back to the "corporate life" I wanted.

Eventually, one of those lights did become my office. It didn't have a window and it was actually a cubicle, but it was a space—my space to continue my journey towards my dream. I was hired as a business analyst at a retailer headquartered in Seattle. My job didn't look too close to what I had envisioned, but I didn't let that distract me. I had a lot to learn and I knew that this, too, was a step toward the HR business world.

Eighteen years later, at that same company, and after taking several different types of roles, I have the job of my dreams. The route has not been linear. It has challenged every centimeter of my perseverance. It has required me to trust my inner truth and not let other voices (both within me and from others) confuse me. I've had to overcome my own insecurities and doubts about how I may not be good enough, strong enough, or *American* enough to achieve what I want. I've been selective in what I receive from people's feedback about how I *am* "too passionate, too direct," while never forgetting that I am enough; I am *more* than enough. Once someone told me that one of my biggest barriers to climbing the ladder was my very thick accent. They asked what language I spoke at home. My family's primary languages are Spanish and French. Sometimes we speak Portuguese, and every once in a while, we speak English. They recommended that I speak only English. I disagreed.

"Spanish and French are an important part of our family heritage and a critical component of our cultures, we want to make sure we pass to the other generations," I explained. "You and I are speaking English right now and you understand me, correct? So please bear with the accent."

To avoid sabotaging my inner voice, I remind myself that many of those comments are well-intended, but sometimes rooted in ignorance, misunderstanding, and a lack of interaction with others who are different from them.

I choose to not get distracted. I stay true to my purpose and my dreams, and don't let the biases nor myself block the way. If somebody tells me, "Your accent is too strong," I reply, "Yes, it is. Now let me show you my ideas for the project at hand." If we don't take comments like this personally, they simply become noise until they diminish and eventually disappear. In my experience, if we start an argument with the speaker, it will only make them fortify their position. Instead, I choose to observe and let it pass to defuse the situation. In the words of author and activist Shane Clairborne, "Peace making doesn't mean passivity. It is the act of interrupting injustice without mirroring injustice, the act of disarming evil without destroying the evildoer, the act of finding a third way that is neither fight nor flight but the careful, arduous pursuit of reconciliation and justice."

CONTINUED GROWTH

My determination hasn't ended now that I've reached my dream job. Frankly, the higher I've climbed in the corporate world, the lonelier it gets. That is especially true in HR. I can't share the stories I hear from my staff with anybody on my team—everything is confidential. I can't really ask for advice either, because I am the one who guides them. It is not easy, and I've learned that it's normal to feel that way. I have understood that I need to be very comfortable with myself, know my values and understand my boundaries.

In the last few years, I have realized the importance of cultivating one's mind and nurturing one's soul to better serve others. I have seen that when my purpose comes across in my work, magical things can happen. My ability to impact others exponentially amplifies. Then the sky is the limit! I am in full alignment: my work and my purpose respond to what I am here to do, and those around us and the companies where we work serve as support systems. For me, my employer is my backdrop, the scenario where I play my life's role. I am fortunate that I have found the right backdrop where I can really make a difference!

Now that I have reached one of my biggest goals—I am the HR leader for Latin America for a U.S. company. I look up and think about what my next "light" is. My next "window" is now the opportunity to help others so that they can help others. It's facilitating that multiplying effect, because I do understand that it's not easy. I have experienced it firsthand, and I know it's even harder for others.

My goal is twofold. First, I want to continue excelling at

my job. It allows me to do the innovative projects that help improve our communities and contribute to the business growth so that we can offer more jobs. Additionally, I want to be closer to people's journeys by sharing my experience and helping them unlock their potential and achieve their dreams through coaching.

While I have made sure that I follow my inner voice with determination and commitment, I also believe that as we go through our journey, we should be opening doors for others. My new destination is how I can help more Latinas and Latinos so that they can enter positions of power and open doors to others.

I am reminded of the person who recruited me for that first job at my current company. Her father was an immigrant from Mexico. She was aware of some of the struggles that I faced at the time of the interview. Later she told me, "You had all the credentials to do the job, you had the passion, and I wanted to give you a chance." Now, it's time for me to pay it forward. While others will need to do the hard work of dreaming and staying consistent to their goals, I want to be on the other side to help them get there.

REFLECT AND RISE

Here are some of my thoughts about getting ahead in the corporate world.

- **Prepare.** Many of us tend to be very good at improvising. Sometimes we just wing it, and then we feel that we need to prove ourselves by offering lots of details about how we have worked hard and have knowledge. Instead, plan the conversation that you will have tomorrow. Think about your agenda and how you are going to influence your audience. Prepare the message. Structure it. Select the three main topics you want to convey. Then let it sit and be quiet. Trust that silence. Improvisation is a good tool to have in your back pocket, but it should never be your main strategy.

- **Fake it until you make it.** I didn't understand this expression for the longest time. I found it frivolous, and it bothered me. Then I understood that you fake it to yourself; you don't fake it to others. And by faking it, you are reprogramming your brain. I fake that I am a great public speaker. I convince myself of it. I put myself out there and stand in front of an audience as an expert public speaker. Eventually my brain believes it, and it becomes true.

- **Don't get distracted.** Don't let external noises steal the energy you will need to achieve your goals. Be clear on your purpose. If HR can help you fulfill it, you've found your light.

BIOGRAPHY

Isabel Montes is Colombian and came to the U.S. twenty years ago. Isabel earned a bachelor's degree as an industrial engineer from Universidad Javeriana and received a master's degree in human resources from Chapman University. She is certified as an ICF Professional Certified Coach.

She is currently the human resources and learning leader for Latin America at a coffee retail chain, having the privilege to lead the employee experience in twenty-one countries. In her role, she is responsible for establishing the vision, goals, and selecting steps that will enable the region to achieve a sustainable competitive advantage through Innovation, Insight, and Inclusion.

She is the mother of two beautiful children, ages two and four, and the wife of an amazing French man, who has brought a whole set of discoveries for her. For the last thirteen years, Isabel has lived in Miami, a city that she loves.

Isabel Montes

Human Resources & Learning Director

Years in HR: 20

isabelmontescoach@gmail.com

Instagram: isamontescoach

RESOURCES:

To achieve any dream, we believe it takes a village. As you look into ways to grow your HR career, consider getting involved in any of the organizations below nationally or locally. They each have programs, events and resources that will help develop your skills for any role. Many of the contributing authors in this book are connected to each of these fantastic organizations that continue to open doors for the Latino community in HR.

- Association of Latino Professionals For America (ALPFA): https://www.alpfa.org
- Chicago United: https://www.chicago-united.org
- Congressional Hispanic Caucus Institute (CHCI): https://chci.org
- Diversity Best Practices: https://www.diversitybestpractices.com
- DiversityInc: https://www.diversityinc.com
- DiversityMBAMagazine: https://diversitymbamagazine.com
- Fig Factor Foundation: https://www.thefigfactor.org
- Hispanic Alliance for Career Enhancement (HACE): https://www.haceonline.org
- Hispanic Association of Colleges & Universities (HACU): https://www.hacu.net

- Hispanic Association on Corporate Responsibility: https://www.hacr.org
- Hispanic Executive: https://hispanicexecutive.com
- Hispanic Inspiring Students' Performance and Achievement (HISPA): https://www.hispa.org
- Hispanic Star: https://hispanicstar.org
- Human Resource Certification Institute (HRCI): https://www.hrci.org
- Human Rights Campaign (HRC): https://www.hrc.org
- Latinas Rising Up In Human Resources Network: https://latinasrisingupinhr.com
- Latino Corporate Directors Association (LCDA): https://latinocorporatedirectors.org
- Latino Leaders Magazine: https://www.latinoleadersmagazine.com
- League of United Latin American Citizens (LULAC): https://lulac.org
- National Association of Women Business Owners (NAWBO): https://www.nawbo.org
- National Hispanic Corporate Council (NHCC): https://www.nhcchq.org
- Network of Executive Women (NEW): https://www.newonline.org

- Prospanica (Association of Hspanic MBAs & Business Professionals): https://www.prospanica.org

- Society of Human Resource Management (SHRM): https://www.shrm.org

- The Latinista: https://www.thelatinista.com

- The Latino Hive: http://www.thelatinohive.com

- UnidosUS: https://www.unidosus.org

- United States Hispanic Chamber of Commerce: https://ushcc.com

- We Are All Human: https://www.weareallhuman.org

- Working Mother Media: https://www.workingmother.com/about-us